UNITED STATES

MILITARY RAILWAY SERVICE

America's Soldier-Railroaders in WWII

UNITED STATES

MILITARY RAILWAY SERVICE

America's Soldier-Railroaders in WWII

Don DeNevi and Bob Hall

A BOSTON MILLS PRESS BOOK

Photographs provided by the Railway Negative Exchange unless otherwise noted.

Canadian Cataloguing in Publication Data

DeNevi, Don, 1937 -
    U.S. Military Railway Service

Includes bibliographical references.
ISBN 1-55046-021-8

1. United States. Army, Transportation Corps.
2. Military railroads – History – 20th century.
I. Hall, Bob 1939 -   . II. Title.

D795.U6D45 1991   940.54'1273   C91-093737-0

© Don DeNevi and Bob Hall, 1992

First published in 1992 by
Stoddart Publishing Co. Limited
34 Lesmill Road
Toronto, Canada
M3B 2T6

A BOSTON MILLS PRESS BOOK
The Boston Mills Press
132 Main St.
Erin, Ontario
N0B 1T0

Winners of the
Heritage Canada
Communications Award

American Association
for State and Local History
Award Winner

Cover Design by Gill Stead, Guelph
Typography by Lexigraf, Tottenham
Printed in Canada

The publisher gratefully acknowledges the support of The Canada Council,
Ontario Arts Council and Ontario Publishing Centre in the development
of writing and publishing in Canada.

Contents

This book is dedicated to Deno Ghiglieri of Morro Bay, California
and to
Warren Edward "Birney" Miller who appreciated the intrinsic value of things old.

Introduction

By the end of World War I it was clear to military leaders that transportation, particularly the ability to move troops and matériel quickly, would play a decisive role in any future global warfare. Success would not only depend upon the number of soldiers and the quantity of supplies that could be forwarded to and within the overseas commands, but also the timeliness with which they were delivered.

Although the importance of an effective railway service for mass movements in theaters of operations was first demonstrated during the American Civil War, and dramatically substantiated in the First World War, the Army's Military Railway Service (MRS) in January 1939 consisted of only a few reserve units, each composed of personnel employed by its sponsoring commercial railroad. Not until more than two years later did the first MRS unit go on active status. In June 1941 the 711th Railway Operating Battalion was activated at Fort Belvoir, Virginia. Within 45 days the battalion was transferred to Camp Claiborne, Louisiana, to take on the Army's first major railroading task, the construction and operation of a single-track railroad from Camp Claiborne to Camp Polk, a distance of over 50 miles.

On December 8, 1941, when the United States declared war on Japan, the 711th was the only railway operating battalion which had been mobilized. Fortunately, the units on reserve status included 5 railway grand divisions, 20 railway operating battalions, and 3 railway shop battalions. In April 1942 the activation of additional units began.

The first three months of the Pacific and European conflicts brought about marked changes in the organization of Army transportation. New agencies were established by President Franklin D. Roosevelt in order to exercise strict control over the strategic deployment of the nation's domestic transportation resources. Although the machinery for handling its transportation requirements was completely resystematized, the organization of the MRS during this early period was based upon the proven principles of successful commercial railroading. In the months and years that followed, modifications were instituted as railroading experience dictated.

In March 1942 the urgent coordination of ships, railway cars, and motor vehicles within the armed forces and the civilian agencies resulted in the creation of the Army Transportation Corps under a Chief of Transportation. Prior to this development, all military transportation had been the responsibility of the Quartermaster General under the supervision of the Supply Division (G-4) of the War Department General Staff. By July 1942 all major policies and decisions affecting transportation were at last Army policies. Although the transportation set-up now began humming more efficiently than ever before, the ensuing adjustments fell short of the ideal. One of the more successful adjustments however, was the transfer of the Military Railway Service from the jurisdiction of the Chief of Engineers to that of the newly created Chief of Transportation. And, with the invasion of North Africa, the MRS received its first combat test.

By the conclusion of hostilities with Germany and Japan, the Military Railway Service had established an enviable record wherever it had functioned overseas. The service's success was attributed chiefly to the fact that not only had a large proportion of the officers and enlisted men been railroaders in civilian life, but most of their units had been trained by large American railroad companies, as well. The 1,161 railroad men who served as MRS officers between 1942 and 1946 had an average of 12 years' railroading experience each, while the 24,374 enlisted men averaged more than 2½ years each. The total strength of the Military Railway Service on June 30, 1945, was 44,084 officers and men, of whom 43,231 served overseas and 853 (a railway operating battalion recalled from Alaska) were in training status in the United States. Of these men, 28,828 served in the European Theater of Operations;

3,207 in the Mediterranean Theater; 3,473 in the Persian Gulf Command; 4,036 in the India-Burma Theater; 2,772 in the Southwest Pacific Area; and 915 in the Alaskan Department.

The illustrated history that follows acclaims the heroism of G.I. railroaders in moving gargantuan amounts of freight and large numbers of troops, often under intense fire and bombardment, over impossible railroads, with motive power that in the United States would have been relegated to the scrap heap half a century before. Cited along with the clerks, telegraph operators, and others who outside normal lines of duty voluntarily manned switch engines to move cars of explosives and inflammables away from other cars that had been set ablaze by enemy action, are the managers who brilliantly planned and coordinated the services' daily operations. For example, prior to the North African invasion, officers prepared seven major railway reports, including detailed railroad maps of various nations in which the service was expected to operate. So thoroughly did these officers carry out their assignment, that when the invasion of France took place, followed by the subsequent overrunning of Germany, the MRS had a detailed map over 40 feet in length, a map which was so accurate that not once during the movement of the vast amount of supplies to the front did a question of available rail facilities arise. In addition, it was perceptive planning that led to the establishment of car and locomotive erecting shops adjacent to principal supply ports. The new cars could thereby be loaded as fast as they were built (125 per day was the average after the invasion of France), thus preventing the loss of precious days or the waste of valuable engines and man-hours due to the hauling of empty cars.

Other stories focus upon the operation of the White Pass & Yukon Line, where soldier-railroaders encountered temperatures as low as 80 degrees below zero. When that mission was completed, most of the men were spirited off to Iran for the construction and operation of railways in temperatures reaching 140 degrees. Without those lines, manned by American G.I.'s, Marshall Zhukov would not have been able to reach Berlin.

Due to the worldwide nature of Allied military operations, U.S. troops operated railways in Alaska, the Yukon, Morocco, Algeria, Tunisia, Sicily, Corsica, Sardinia, Italy, France, Luxembourg, Austria, Germany, Holland, Belgium, Liechtenstein, Iran, India, Burma and Luzon. In addition, they aided in operations in Egypt and England. By instituting American operating methods and providing modern efficient power, the men of the Military Railway Service accomplished what the peacetime personnel of these countries considered impossible. For example, in Tunisia the MRS took control of a 300-mile meter-gauge line over which the former operators had been able to haul only four 250-ton trains per day. Within 24 hours of assuming control and inaugurating proven practices, the MRS had 12 trains moving in each direction.

Gleaned from base depot company histories, War Department publications, and the American Association of Railroads files, the personal vignettes and eyewitness accounts in this book testify to the largest, most complicated supply operation the world has ever known. Accepting as routine the hazards of bombing, strafing and sniping, train crews in combat roles not only hastily repaired tracks and shaky bridges, but willingly hauled troops and supplies to forward railheads in ever-increasing volume until the nation's enemies in Europe and the Pacific crumbled under the weight of Allied power.

The authors wish to acknowledge the most frequently quoted sources of background information in the compiling of the following story. These were the hundreds of articles which appeared in *Railway Age* magazine during the course of World War II, each report or story following closely the events and details of the Military Railway Service in action. Also acknowledged is the Office of the Chief of Military History volume *The United States Army in World War II: The Technical Services—Transportation Corps*.

The following story chronicles the courage, ingenuity and resourcefulness of the G.I.'s who made up the Military Railway Service.

I

Birth of a Remarkable Service

When the United States began offensive operations for the first time in mid-1942, top military strategists in the War Department knew that successful advances would be dependent upon strong lines of supplies and communications. They were, therefore, greatly gratified their Army had not overlooked the critical importance of the rail service—that is, efficient, no-nonsense railroad companies at home, and tough, well-trained railway construction and operating battalions in the field.

Throughout the homefront, the railroad companies, under private management, had scored phenomenal successes in transporting troops and tonnage to coastal embarkation points. And while compiling unprecedented records, the railways mobilized thousands of their employees for service as officers and engineers in the numerous branches of the fighting forces. By the time Guadalcanal was captured, railway battalions were being organized throughout America, under the guidance of the newly established Military Railway Service. Inducted and trained as compact operating units, these highly capable troops were readied for duty within, or behind, any theater of operation assigned.

But who were these soldier-railroaders? What was the Military Railway Service? Where did the idea originate?

In 1830, on the opening of the Liverpool & Manchester Railway in England, a British regiment was transported 38 miles in less than two hours, as opposed to more than two days of marching. It didn't require genius for Army commanders to realize that rail transport could exert a determining influence in future wars. In Germany, a few years later, Frederick Wilhelm Harkot, a civil engineer who had participated in the Napoleonic Wars, drafted a plan to construct a railroad connecting the Wesser River with the Lippe, lecturing on its special military value. German High Command was impressed by the idea of building railways for future offensive operations, that by 1845 it had laid some 3,500 miles of track, compared to only 1,000 miles in France. By the following year, Prussia's 6th Army Corps, consisting of some 12,000 men, together with horses, carriages, guns and ammunition, had been shipped over two railway lines to Cracow, Poland. And in 1849 a Russian corps of more than 30,000 men, with all its equipment, was dispatched by rail from its cantonment in eastern Poland to Goding, Czechoslovakia, to join the Austrian Army. But the largest movement of troops recorded during this period occurred in the early winter of 1850. More than 75,000 troops, 8,000 horses and 1,000 carriages of the Austrian Army were transported from Vienna and Hungary to the Silesian Frontier.

Historians are generally agreed that the first effective military use of the railroads occurred during the American Civil War. Within an area of military operations almost the size of Europe, the American railroad engineer held the key to potential victory. The Union, determined to reclaim the seceded Southern States, took possession of the Philadelphia-Wilmington-Baltimore Railway on March 31, 1861. At first, however, both Union and Confederate generals were reluctant to distance themselves from their supply bases if it meant depending on railroads. In the South, tracks were not only inadequate, but most of the roads were impassable during the winter's rainy season. Gauges varied from 6 feet to narrow gauge. Ties were usually round logs or, at best, rough-hewn timber. Iron of every imaginable shape and weight made up the primitive rails. Raiding cavalry parties from the North had little trouble destroying miles of lines in relatively short time. Throughout the first year of the Civil War, no railway maintenance or reconstruction teams existed in either the North or the South.

President Abraham Lincoln realized that, as the chief means of supplying the Union's Army of the Potomac, the railroads in the North had to be under the absolute control of the military authorities in Washington, D.C. In late January 1862 Congress authorized the President, at his discretion, to take possession of and place under military control the nation's telegraph lines and railroads. This law, in essence, was the first authorized conscription of personnel and property in the United States. The railroad companies, patriotically sympathetic with the Union cause, cooperated fully.

Lincoln also recognized that it would soon be necessary for an experienced railroad executive to assume the responsibility for railway operations in the "soon-to-be-occupied" Southern states. On February 11, 1862, Secretary of War Edwin Stanton, under the President's specific order, appointed Daniel Craig McCallum, General Superintendent of the Erie Railroad, as the "Military Director and Superintendent of Railroads in the United States." McCallum became a brigadier general with extraordinary powers.

The details of the issuing order are interesting because they spell the birth of the Military Railway Service in the United States Army:

Washington City, February 11, 1862.

Ordered that D.C. McCallum, be and he hereby is, appointed Military Director and Superintendent of Railroads in the United States, with authority to enter upon, take possession of, hold and use all railroads, engines, cars, locomotives, equipment, appendages, and appurtenances that may be required for the transport of troops, army, ammunition and military supplies of the United States, and to do and perform all acts and things that may be necessary and proper to be done for the safe and speedy transport aforesaid. By order of the President, Commander in Chief of the Army and Navy of the United States, Edwin M. Stanton, Secretary of War.

A man of driving energy and perseverance, McCallum created an organization which would have striking similarities to the Military Railway Service established in 1941. Although the Brigadier General was eventually successful in supervising 2,105 miles of railroad for the federal government, he had to tackle innumerable early problems. For example, his scheduling of trains was constantly interfered with, while his direct orders were often rescinded by local military commanders who insisted they could wage their battles without the assistance of "mere railroad men." On one occasion, an urgently needed troop train was delayed for several hours while a general's wife did some shopping. An infuriated McCallum quickly brought such incompetence and neglect to an abrupt halt by issuing a strongly worded order requiring immediate unloading, protection and, most imperative of all, non-interference of scheduling by anyone not connected with the newly created Military Railway Service.

Another problem was reminiscent of that faced during World War II: various gauges, from narrow to six-foot. Wisely, McCallum divided his forces into a Transportation Department and a Construction Department. Later he would issue orders procuring locomotives and cars. The following quotation from an article entitled "Recollections of Secretary Stanton," which appeared in the March 1887 issue of *Century* magazine, vividly illustrates the role played by the railroads during the conduct of the war:

The defeat of Rosecrans, at Chickamauga, was believed to imperil East Tennessee, and the Secretary of War was urged to send a strong reinforcement there from the Army of the Potomac. General Halleck, Commander in Chief of the Army of the United States, contended that it was impossible to get an effective reinforcement there in time; and the President, after hearing both sides, accepted the judgment of Halleck. Mr. Stanton put off the decision till evening, when he and General Halleck were to be ready with details to support their conclusions. The Secretary then sent for General McCallum, who was neither a lawyer nor a strategist, but a master of railway science. He (Mr. Stanton) showed how many officers, men, horses, and pieces of artillery and how much baggage it was proposed to move from the Rapidan to Tennessee, and asked him (McCallum) to name the shortest time he would undertake to do it in if his life depended on it.

McCallum made some rapid calculations, jotted down some projects connected with the move, and named a time within that which Halleck had admitted would be soon enough, if it were only

Another Civil War first was the development of rail-carried mortars like this one used in the Virginia campaigns.
– *Norfolk Southern Corp.*

View of roundhouse, Alexandria, Va., Orange & Alexandria Railroad during the War Between the States. (From the book *The Southern Railway System* by William Webb, published by The Boston Mills Press.)
– *Norfolk Southern Corp.*

Wrecks were a frequent occurence on the O&A during the war years. Part of it was operated by Federal forces as the U.S. Military RR., part operated for the Confederacy. It was a railroad divided.
– *Norfolk Southern Corp.*

The 13-inch mortar shown was named "The Dictator." It was used by the Federal artillery around Petersburg during the closing months of the war.   – *Norfolk Southern Corp.*

possible; this time being conditioned on his (McCallum's) being able to control everything that he could reach. The Secretary was delighted, told him (McCallum) he would make him a Brigadier General the day the last train was safely unloaded; put him on his mettle by telling him of Halleck's assertion that the thing was beyond human power; told him to go to work and work out final calculations and projects, and to begin preliminary measures, using his (Mr. Stanton's) name and authority everywhere; and finally instruct him what to do and say when he (Mr. Stanton) should send for him by and by to come over to the Department. When the conference was resumed and McCallum was introduced, his apparently spontaneous demonstrations of how easily and surely the impossible thing could be done convinced the two skeptics, and the movement was ordered and made and figures now in military science as a grand piece of strategy.

That "grand piece of strategy" meant transporting more than 23,000 men, their equipment and supplies 1,200 miles in less than seven days.

At the conclusion of the Civil War, the German General Staff, having carefully observed the role played by railroads in defeating the Confederacy, initiated a "Field Railway Section" of railroad troops. France did likewise and, in 1870-1871 railways played an influencing part in the Franco-Prussian War. England, also sensitive to the role of rapid rail transportation, organized railroad battalions and used them in the Boer War between 1899 and 1902.

Lessons Learned in World War I

After the Civil War ended in 1865, the U.S. Army retired to frontier posts in order to protect westbound settlers from the Indians. Only animal transport was necessary beyond the extensions of the commercial railroads. While the enterprising German militarists were organizing permanent railway construction, operating corps, full-fledged training centers, and the training of railroad reservists, American Army planners saw little need for similar actions. But in June 1916, while mobilizing U.S. troops on the Mexican border, General William M. Black, Chief of Engineers, realized that nothing had been done to establish an effective military railway service since 1865, and he called upon the nation's private railroads for assistance.

On June 24, 1916, Black wired Samuel M. Felton, President of the Chicago Great Western, and asked him to organize, maintain and operate railroads south of the Rio Grande. Felton's new title was Consulting Engineer and Adviser to the Chief of Engineers. The idea was to recruit transportation officers from civilian positions, earmark material to construct 150 miles of railroad, and designate the personnel to maintain and operate those 150 miles by the border. Within two weeks the request was fulfilled, although the men and material were no longer required. The U.S. Chiefs of Staff, however, asked Felton to continue serving because of possible American intervention in World War I, which was currently raging in Western Europe. On February 3, 1917, the government ordered the establishment of the 3rd Engineers (later known as the 13th), with its personnel recruited from six Chicago railroads, one company from each. On May 14, 1917, War Department General Order No. 61 authorized eight additional railroad regiments, of which five would be assigned to construction, three to operations, and one to shop. The order stipulated that the Colonel and the Regimental Adjutant were to be Regular Army officers, with the remainder of the officers to be selected from railroad personnel.

Thus, by the time the United States entered the war on April 6, 1917, significant strides had been taken to ensure war-ready railroad regiments. By August the Army had dispatched to France 20 military operating regiments, 6 maintenance-of-way regiments, 8 car regiments, and 12 locomotive shop regiments. Felton's office, which had begun with one engineer officer and three clerks, had by now expanded to 102 officers, 118 enlisted men, and 57 civilians. Overall American strength by November 30, 1918, would reach 897 railway officers commanding 32,149 soldier-railroaders. In addition, the Transportation Service would at one time or another control over 20,000 stevedoring and inland waterway troops.

The premier accomplishments of America's Military Railway Service in World War I included the standardization, as far as possible, of all railroad equipment, the acceleration of production, and the reduction of costs, resulting in a savings of over $33 million. The first request for locomotives from France was for 300. Each was to be of a consolidation type of 35,600 pounds tractive effort, weighing 166,400 pounds, having 21-by-28-inch cylinders, and 56-inch driving wheels. The Baldwin Locomotive Works in the United States was ordered to devote their entire capacity to standard-gauge locomotives for overseas use. The initial engine was assembled within 20 working days, and Baldwin's ultimate capacity would reach 300 engines per month. In total, 3,400 were ordered. Meanwhile, the American Locomotive Company, Baldwin's chief competitor, would continue to produce engines exclusively for home use.

In France, Brigadier General W.W. Atterbury, formerly a chief executive of the Pennsylvania Railroad, directed the U.S. Transportation Service, administering 13 grand divisions forward and 6 in the rear. By 1918 Atterbury's railroad troops were placed under the Commanding General of Services and Supply.

Although the Transportation Service distinguished itself throughout bitter, costly campaigns, the French General Staff was quick to criticize American railway practices as clumsy and overmanned. Some soldier-railroaders were said to have been out of control, having forcibly ejected French pilots assigned to their locomotives. This may have been true. Certainly it was common knowledge that when the Armistice was announced on November 11, 1918, American crews abandoned their trains in stations, sidings, and on the main tracks to join in the general merriment.

With the passage of the National Defense Act of 1920, a skeleton force of the Transportation Service was organized. Although the act's provisions would never be fully carried out, the 1920s witnessed the establishment of an Officer's Reserve Corps, whose members would form the bulk of the Army officer personnel on December 7, 1941. Thus, the basic structure of the Military Railway Service, which had been battle-tested in the latter stages of World War I, was revived by the Chief of Engineers. Learning from the experience gained in France, the railway operating battalion was reintroduced as the core unit. Some 32 of these battalions would be established by the United States trunk lines. Officers would be commissioned from among appropriate managers of sponsoring railroads. Nine "Regular Army Inactive" battalions would also be created, picking up their personnel from experienced railway reserve officers in the various corps areas. One railway shop battalion would be formed by the Big Four at Beach Grove Shops near Indianapolis, Indiana. A grand division would become the responsibility of the Eighth Corps Area. Unfortunately, appropriations were at a minimum. With prosperity and depression, the nation's interest in its military forces waned. Virtually no provisions for advanced training or mobilization in case of war were planned. The Army struggled to hold together what it could. Fortunately the railway units, governed by the officers who had been commissioned for five-year periods by sponsoring railroad companies, continued at near full strength.

With the war in Europe imminent, Colonel J.J. Kingman was appointed Assistant Chief of Engineers with the rank of brigadier general. Upon his arrival in Washington, D.C., he discovered that the fledgling Military Railway Service was existing on little more than the interest and energy of its men. Determined to revitalize the infant service, he persuaded Carl R. Gray Jr., Executive Vice-President of the Chicago, St. Paul, Minneapolis & Omaha Railroad, to serve as his personal consultant in rebuilding the program. Gray immediately went to work. He saw that the service as a whole was not a balanced force and that many of the units were in an unhealthy condition. Gray had no staff to speak of and there were no grant divisions or the intermediate headquarters necessary for wide lateral or axial mobilization. There was only one shop battalion to handle the back shop work for 42 divisions. Within

An American troop train, complete with 36 cars and Baldwin engine, ready to start for Brest from Beaumont-Vivion, Garthe, France, with 28th Division men. (1919)

This 150-ton Baldwin locomotive with American train crew is shown at St. Pierre des Corps, Indre et Loire, France. (circa 1918)

three months of coming aboard, Gray was commissioned as Manager, Military Railway Service, on February 1, 1939, reporting directly to Kingman. Later this brilliant tactician would be promoted to the position of Director General of the Military Railway Service, and he would eventually achieve the rank of major general.

One of Kingman's first actions, upon Gray's recommendation, was to transfer a section of the office of the Chief of Engineers to the Military Railway Service. A second major decision, again at Gray's request, was the appointment of Colonel Charles D. Young, Vice-President of the Pennsylvania, as consultant to the MRS Chief of Engineers. In the event of war, Young would assume all responsibilities for the mobilization staff work in the Chief's office. Gray would assume command in the field. The 1930s ended with Young in charge in Washington, D.C., and Gray personally touring the major railroad companies throughout the nation, impressing upon the chief operating officers the importance of maintaining their reserve fully manned with experienced personnel.

Meanwhile, Gray, Kingman and Young, after careful analysis, decided that 10 grand divisions and 6 shop battalions would be about the minimum needed in the event the United States entered the European conflict. Because it was not feasible to increase the size of these additional units, it was necessary to discontinue, during the current peace, 22 of the operating battalions, and instead concentrate on bringing up to strength Railway Headquarters, 5 grand divisions, and 3 shop battalions. The 22 discontinued operating battalions would be immediately mobilized by the sponsoring railroads. Although the geographical distribution was not ideal, the units were thickest where there were the most railroads.

Thus, when the Japanese attacked Pearl Harbor, the organization of the Military Railway Service was as follows:

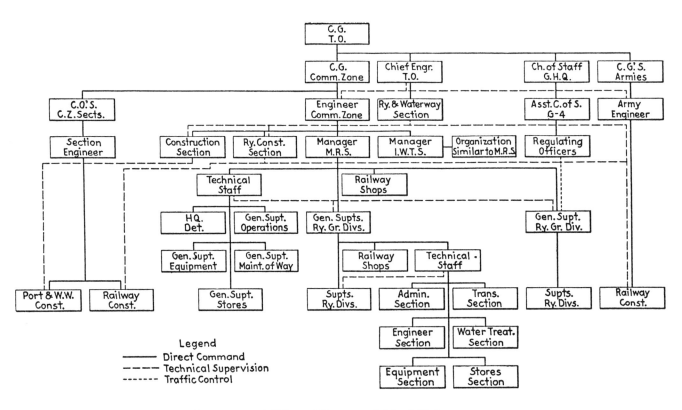

Organization of Military Railways and Inland Waterways

Although the military railways were an engineer supply organization functioning under the Commanding General, Communications Zone, through his engineer, the basic unit for transportation and maintenance remained the operating battalion on a small railway division of 75 to 100 miles, depending of course upon the density of traffic to be handled.

The Operating Battalions

Within a week after Pearl Harbor, the United States had ready for duty one railway operating battalion, which was activated as part of the regular Army currently in training on the Claiborne-Polk Railroad. The division superintendent was a lieutenant colonel and the battalion consisted of 18 line officers and 3 attached medics, for a total of 21 officers, plus 803 enlisted men. The battalion consisted of four companies: a Headquarters Company responsible for dispatching and supplies; Company A for track and signal maintenance, as well as maintenance of way; Company B to operate the roundhouses and maintain all equipment in proper working order; and Company C to serve as the actual operating unit with 50 train crews managed by a trainmaster.

The commander of the battalion, as mentioned, was a division superintendent, and his major served as the assistant division superintendent. A captain was adjutant, although the real commander of the Headquarters and Service Company was the division storekeeper, who was also a captain. The Headquarters Company was in turn divided into a company headquarters, an administrative section, a technical section, a supply and transport section, a mess section, a train movement section (the dispatching unit), and a signal maintenance section. The company consisted of 6 officers and 106 enlisted specialists.

Company A, responsible for track and signal maintenance, as well as maintenance of way, was composed of 4 officers and 190 enlisted men. The company commander was an engineer, maintenance of way, while his other officers consisted of a supervisor of bridges and buildings, a track supervisor, and an assistant engineer, maintenance of way. The company was divided into two platoons, one a bridge-and-building-maintenance platoon and the other a track-maintenance platoon. Company B, the equipment maintenance company, consisted of 4 officers and 182 enlisted men. The company commander was a master mechanic, one officer was a mechanical engineer, another was an enginehouse foreman, and the fourth was a general or foreman. This company was also divided into two platoons, one a car-repair platoon and the other a locomotive-repair platoon. Company C, the transportation company, consisted of 4 officers and 325 enlisted men. This company commander, a trainmaster, was supported by two lieutenant travelling engineers, or road foremen of engines, while the fourth officer was the yardmaster. Company C consisted of two train-operating platoons with 25 train crews in each platoon.

The engineer battalion, Railway Shop, of which three were authorized, was strictly a back-shop organization. The commander held the rank of lieutenant colonel and served as the general shop superintendent. This group consisted of a Battalion Headquarters, Headquarters and Service Company, Company A (erecting and machine shop), Company B (boiler and blacksmith shop), and Company C (car-repair shop). There were 23 officers and 658 enlisted men in this unit, including 3 attached medical officers and 16 enlisted medical men.

By 1942 American railroads were generously cooperating by accepting sponsorship or affiliation of units. These were the Santa Fe (four units); Atlantic Coast Line; Baltimore & Ohio; Boston & Maine; Central of Georgia; Central Railroad of New Jersey (in conjunction with the Reading); Chesapeake & Ohio; Chicago & North Western; Chicago, Burlington & Quincy; Chicago Great Western; Chicago, Milwaukee, St. Paul & Pacific; Chicago, St. Paul, Minneapolis & Omaha; Big Four (two units); Denver & Rio Grande Western; Erie, Great Northern (two units); Illinois Central (two units); Lehigh Valley, Louisville & Nashville; Missouri-Kansas-Texas; Missouri Pacific; New York Central (four units); New York, New Haven & Hartford (two units); Norfolk & Western; Northern Pacific; Pennsylvania (six

Narrow-gauge locomotives used to transport troops at Langley Ridge, Fort Benning, GA. (7-28-41)

units); Reading, St. Louis-San Francisco; Seaboard Air Line; Southern (two units); Southern Pacific (five units); Texas & Pacific; Union Pacific (four units); and the Wabash.

In accepting sponsorship and affiliation with the 5 railway grand division headquarters, the 20 operating battalions, and the 3 shop battalions, the railroads asked their selected officers to recommend appropriate assignments for themselves. However, for the other 5 grand division headquarters, 22 operating battalions, and 3 shop battalions, the carriers would simply furnish railroad officer personnel for commissioning.

The 711th Engineer Battalion Constructs the Claiborne & Polk Military Railway

The first organized railway battalion in the United States Army was the 711th Engineer Battalion, Railway Operating, which had been activated on July 18, 1941, some 7½ months prior to the surprise attack at Pearl Harbor. Within 48 days of its organization, the small nucleus of trained officers and men had completely rehabilitated the 4½ mile Quartermaster Railroad serving Ft. Belvoir in Virginia. The work involved replacing thousands of ties, installing 7,000 tie plates, rebuilding or repairing several bridges, installing 20 culverts, and the relining and surfacing of the entire line, including the placing of 9,000 cubic yards of ballast. But this was a small accomplishment compared to the 711th's second achievement, the construction out of face of a 50-mile military railroad between Camps Claiborne and Polk in Louisiana.

The construction of such a line was a remarkable achievement, one of which any long-standing, well-trained railway organization would have been proud. It was constructed by the Corps of Engineers to serve as a proving ground, or training railroad, for thousands of men serving in the operating battalions of the Military Railway Service. The driving of the golden spike on July 11, 1942, marked the completion of the first Army-built, strictly military railroad in the history of the nation. As Brigadier General Carl R. Gray Jr., the general manager of the MRS, stated at the time, "More important, the completion of this railroad demonstrates what the Military Railway Service can do in theaters of military operation, if called upon."

The story of the Claiborne & Polk Military Railway is about a railroad that most experts believed couldn't be built, except at exorbitant cost and in the face of major difficulties. This remarkable line was constructed in spite of these difficulties by an organization created to operate and maintain an existing railroad, rather than one schooled in construction. Further- more, the Claiborne & Polk amassed its own motive power and rolling stock, and continued operating throughout World War II and after, under military personnel organized on a typical railroad division basis.

As might be expected, the line was not constructed to trunk-line standards in terms of rails, grades and alignment. Slightly less than 50 miles in length, the railroad extended in a general east-west direction, with Camp Claiborne at the east end and Camp Polk at the west end. Traversing primarily low-lying country, the railroad undulated with a ruling grade of two percent in each direction, one-half of one percent heavier than had been originally anticipated, the change having been made during the course of the work in order to minimize grading and speed up completion. Except for five curves of six degrees to meet special conditions, maximum curvature on the line was no more than four degrees.

Local civilian engineers claimed the construction of the railroad, especially its western half, was impracticable. For the 711th Engineer Battalion, the project presented a challenge. The officers and men were not seeking a line that would be easy to build, maintain and operate; they wanted something that would afford maximum experience in all of the varied aspects of railroading.

More than 6,000 troops participated in the line's construction. In general, the line was laid out to follow the contours of the ground as much as possible. In addition, engineers were mindful that, under military regulations, train operations on the railroad would seldom exceed 30 to 35 miles an hour. With few exceptions, fills had a maximum height of 20 feet, while cut depths were seldom more than 15 feet. By following the higher contours, pipe culverts sufficed instead of bridges, and the total grading was kept to approximately 600,000 cubic yards. Final standards called for subgrade widths of 16 feet on fills and 20 feet in cuts, with 1½-to-1-foot side slopes in both cases, although these standards were sacrificed at many points for speed during construction.

Track construction consisted of 75- and 80-pound second-hand rail throughout. The ties were of a wide variety of woods, generally 6 by 8 inches by 8 or 8½ feet. About 60 percent were treated with creosote and about 75 percent, including all of those on curves, were equipped with second-hand tie plates. In the interest of speed, the ties were laid as received, without regard for segregation of treated and untreated varieties. Ballast throughout the line was of pit-run gravel, including about 40 percent sand, the ultimate goal being to place 6 to 8 inches of this material beneath the ties.

At the onset, the 711th started grading with no spikes, bolts, tie plates, spring washers or turnouts, and no locomotives. More important, the battalion had no earth-moving equipment. When work began on the main line, the 711th had to rent two tractor bulldozers from a local contractor. Soon, however, the first Army grading equipment began to arrive. Included were nine 9-yard tractor-scraper units, three 12-yard tractor-scraper units, four 6-yard tractor-scraper units, eight tractor bulldozers, and four draglines, supplemented by a large number of trucks. All were used on the soil, most of which included sand, muck and gumbo, with interspersed layers of quicksand. A longer-than-normal rainy season, which at one point saw a downpour of over 9 inches in 30 hours, added to the difficulties faced by the battalion. Tractors and trucks were bogged down. At certain places, the draglines, operating on corduroy roadways by the center line of track, were the only feasible means of building fills.

Day after day the engineer troops of the 711th, assisted by the troops of several General Service Engineer battalions, pushed ahead, working from both ends of the line toward the middle. During one period work was under way at 25 points, commanders taking advantage of the troops and equipment available and jumping from one point to another, seeking the most favorable conditions at the moment. At many points, the natural ground was so soft that in order to sustain the fill it was necessary to support it on a solid log instead of building over the ground surface. At other points, large logs laid end to end along the toes of the embankment were used to confine deep embankment footings of coarse sand brought in for the purpose. At still other points, timber cribbing was the only practicable recourse to get across the low-lying soft spots. In addition, all along the route there were rattlesnakes to bother the troopers as they laid 250 to 300 rails a day.

The soldiers worked without power tools such as pneumatic spike-drivers and pneumatic wrenches. Often working under a blazing sun, with high humidity and temperatures in excess of 110 degrees, the men built inward from the east and west railheads, from early morning until 10 p.m. Perhaps the most remarkable aspect of their incredible achievement was the construction of 25 bridges. This phase was not outstanding because of the large number of bridges built (actually, the number had been reduced from 50), but rather because of the generally high standards of material and workmanship employed in spite of the fact that the majority of the troops had little or no prior experience in bridge construction or any form of heavy timber work. The longest bridge on the line extruded over the Calcosieu River and was 2,126 feet long and made up of 4- and 5-post bents. The maximum height of the structure above the ground level was approximately 15 feet.

On July 10 the 50-mile single-track line connecting Camps Claiborne and Polk in Louisiana was completed. The following morning, in a ceremony witnessed by several thousand members of the 711th Engineer Battalion and assisting units, Brigadier General Carl R.

In support of 3rd Army maneuvers at Camp Polk, LA, M-3 tanks were checked upon arrival at Boyce, LA. (8-28-42)

Gray Jr. drove a golden spike in the final rail. Following this, on the 11th day of the 7th month, locomotives Nos. 7 and 11, significant of the 711th Battalion, were brought to a coupling over that last rail, where the commanders of Camps Claiborne and Polk, standing on the pilot steps of the two locomotives, saluted and joined hands, not only marking one of the most successful railroad accomplishments in the history of the U.S. Armed Forces, but also the beginning of America's first proving ground for thousands of men in the Army Railway Service.

As a postscript to this remarkable story, it should be noted that the operation and maintenance of the line would be handled entirely by the 711th Battalion, organized on a military-divisional basis. This meant that the battalion would be broken up into a group of general officers and four companies, each man in each company having an appropriate military rating and duties. The organization would be similar to that in effect on the individual operating divisions of most Class 1 railroads.

The equipment available to the 711th included 7 oil-burning 79-ton ten-wheelers secured from the Texas & Pacific Railway; 2 new oil-burning 85-ton consolidation-type locomotives obtained from the Lima Locomotive Works; 2 coaches and 2 combination cars; 16 box cars; 50 flat cars; 25 gondola cars; 12 tank cars; and 4 refrigerator cars. In addition, 4 box cars and 2 refrigerator cars were converted into cabooses by the mechanical units of the 711th. The cabooses were equipped with side bay windows instead of the conventional top cupolas. Furthermore, these units would handle car repairs as well as locomotive running repairs. For Class 1, 2 and 3 repairs, the locomotive parts, or the complete locomotives, would be turned over to one of the railway equipment maintenance battalions being organized in the United States at the time. Since the railway had no manual or automatic block signals, it would be operated entirely by train order, employing a push-button-type automatic-selector telephone system with stations at both terminals and intermediate points along the way. During the initial year of operations, the commanding officer of the 711th Battalion and superintendent of the Claiborne & Polk Railway was Lieutenant Colonel G.M. Welch, formerly Assistant Division Superintendent of the Chicago, St. Paul, Minneapolis & Omaha, based in St. James, Minnesota.

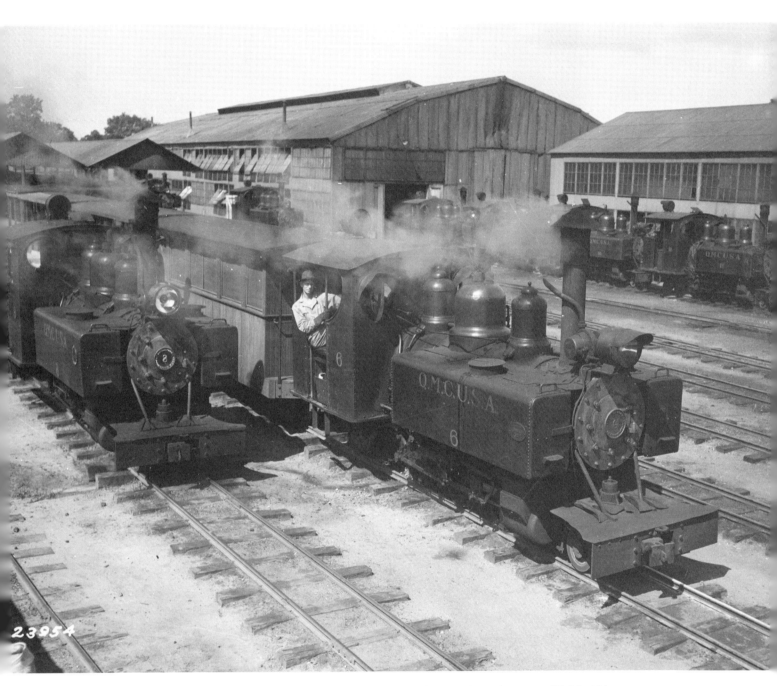

A locomotive of the 60cm narrow-gauge railroad at Ft. Benning, GA. (7-25-41)

Sgt. W.J. Overton, Engineer of the 6th White Quartermaster Detachment, oiling wheels at the railroad yards at Ft. Benning, GA. (7-25-41)

A Davenport narrow-gauge locomotive at Fort Benning, GA, pulls a train loaded with logs to a sawmill. (6-26-42)

Members of 502nd Parachute Battalion, as a means of being prepared for "come what may," receive instructions in operating a locomotive. Ft. Benning, Ga. (12-28-41)

In order to be ready for the possibility of commandeering a train behind enemy lines, members of the 502nd Parachute Battalion were instructed at Ft. Benning, GA, in the workings of a locomotive. (12-28-41)

A sergeant from the 502nd Parachute Battalion, sits at the controls of a locomotive during a course of locomotive-operation given parachute troopers. Ft. Benning, Ga. (12-28-41)

This member of the 502nd Parachute Battalion, during a course in locomotive-operations, gives a signal. This training qualifies a parachutist to operate enemy locomotives, if ever the occasion arises. Ft. Benning, Ga. (12-28-41)

Headquarters of the 745th Railway Operating Battalion, Ft. Wayne, IN. (10-16-43)

Salvage officer Capt. Smith Peterson directs the loading of scrap-salvage 15-ton Cristie Convertable tanks from the 10th Armored Division area at Fort Benning, GA. (8-11-42)

Capt. Reuben Whellis of the Transportation Corps, Camp Fannin, TX, tests a diesel engine used in the warehouse area. (1943)

T/5 Carl Smelser is the engineer for a new engine at Camp Bowie, TX. (12-22-42)

A railroad hoist crane is used to lift railroad wheels from a flat car at Ft. Sam Houston, TX. (7-9-43)

Tanks requiring repairs which could not be completed at Camp Polk, LA, were sent back to the factory. (7-8-43)

In support of 3rd Army maneuvers at Camp Polk, LA, an M-3 tank moves down a ramp from flat cars at Boyce, LA. (8-28-42)

Men of the 16th Armored Division loading medium tanks at Camp Chaffee, AR. (6-3-43)

Men of the 716th Railway Operating Battalion put through a "rush check" on an engine in the Southern Pacific yards in San Antonio, TX. (5-11-44)

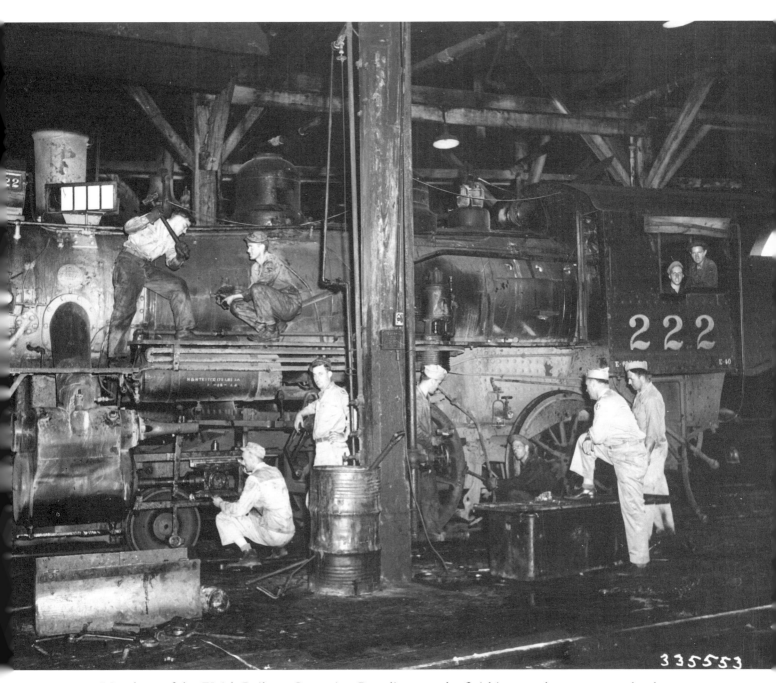

Members of the 716th Railway Operating Battalion put the finishing touches on an overhaul of engine 222 at Fort Sam Houston, TX. (5-11-44)

White Pass & Yukon Railway train entering Scagway, Alaska, terminal after a run from Whitehorse, Yukon Territory, Canada. (December 1942)

II

The Military Railway Service Goes to War

On the morning of December 7, 1941, Japanese Naval and Air Forces made a surprise attack on U.S. Naval and Air bases at Pearl Harbor. Eighteen U.S. warships were sunk or damaged, some 170 planes destroyed, and more than 2,000 Americans were killed. Almost immediately, the United States declared war on Japan. After Germany and Italy declared war on the United States, Congress passed a resolution recognizing a state of war between the United States and these nations.

Within weeks, units of what would soon become the Military Railway Service were called into active service. In January 1942 a contract had been entered into between the railroads, represented by the Association of American Railroads, and the U.S. government, represented by the Chief of Engineers. After basic military training, these various units would be trained on their sponsoring railroads.

The first unit to be called into active service was the 727th Railway Operating Battalion, activated on March 15, 1942, and trained on the Southern Railroad between Meridian and New Orleans. On April 15, 1942, came the activation of the 713th, which trained on the Santa Fe at Clovis, New Mexico, and the 753rd Railway Shop Battalion, which trained in the New York Central Shops at Bucyrus, Ohio. On May 15, 1942, these battalions were followed by Headquarters, 1st Military Railway Service, which trained in the Railroad Center at St. Paul, Minnesota, and the 730th Railway Operation Battalion, which trained on the Fort Wayne Division of the Pennsylvania Railroad. On August 1, 1942, the 703rd Railway Grand Division was activated and trained in company with Headquarters, 1st Military Railway Service at St. Paul. The 703rd Railway Grand Division was organized about September 1, 1942, to consist of the 713th, 727th, and 730th Railway Operating Battalions, and the 753rd Railway Shop Battalion.

During that eventful spring and summer of 1942, officers were trained for a month to six weeks in Transportation Corps schools, then each unit was activated and placed in training on a railroad. The General Manager, Military Railway Service, acting for the Chief of Engineers (until November 15, 1942, when General Orders No. 60 transferred the MRS to the newly created Transportation Corps), was charged with the planning and training of these railway troops as they were called into active service.

The first troops actually sent abroad were in a provisional battalion known as the 770th, which on October 1, 1942, took over the operation of the White Pass & Yukon Railroad in Alaska. Almost at the same time, the 703rd Railway Grand Division was set up and accompanied General Patton as part of his Western Task Force which landed at Casablanca in the autumn of 1942.

Playing Casey Jones at Sixty Below

When the railroad soldiers of the 770th Railway Operating Battalion came down the gang-plank in Skagway's rocky harbor, they knew they were in for the challenge of a lifetime. They were going up against "the toughest, goddamn 110 miles of track in the world." In civilian life, some of the railroaders of the 770th had highballed Southern Pacific trains through the high Sierras, where snow can choke a pass between nightfall and dawn. Others had brought New York Central fliers down the Mohawk Valley in the fiercest blizzards of the eastern seaboard. Still others had stoked freight engines of the Great Northern across the Montana Rockies or braked the Milwaukee's gaudy orange Olympian down the twisting switchbacks of the Bitterroots. There was little question about it: these G.I. railroaders had experience

38

This pipeline on the side of a White Pass & Yukon trestle carried gasoline and oil from the tidewater at Skagway, Alaska, to Whitehorse and Watson Lake, Yukon, Canada, and Fairbanks, Alaska. (Winter 1944-1945)

Opposite: G.I.'s repairing a rotary damaged on the White Pass & Yukon Railway by driving into heavy drifts of snow that was wet when it fell then froze solid. (1944)

Unloading of baggage by enlisted men on the White Pass & Yukon Railway. (December 1942)

With guards stationed at strategic points, a train on the White Pass & Yukon Railway takes on water. (December 1942)

which ran the whole gamut of American railroading. But none of them had ever seen anything to match the 110 narrow-gauge miles of the White Pass & Yukon. One man from the Long Island Railroad in New York said after his first jolting journey over the railroad, "That line's too steep for a goat and too cold for a polar bear."

Yet those 110 miles were vital to the American war effort. For that reason the 770th had been activated and shipped northward by Army transport up the mountain-barricaded waters of the Inside Passage. The White Pass & Yukon afforded the only access to the sub-Arctic solitudes along the 1,630-mile route of the Alaska Highway between Dawson Creek, British Columbia, and Fairbanks, Alaska. It was also the link between the highway and the sea. It was the one place where troops might work on the historic road other than at the terminals, and it offered the only chance to complete the highway on schedule.

The White Pass & Yukon ended in Whitehorse, at the center of the chain of strategic airports between Watson Lake and Northway, tying Alaska by air to the Canadian North. These airports required vast expansion. In addition to all this, the American Army had under way the immense Canol Project, requiring 640 miles of wilderness pipeline to bring the product of the Norman Wells oil fields on the MacKenzie River to the military bases and airports of the North Pacific theater. This meant that thousands of tons of cement, endless miles of pipe, innumerable bulldozers, and huge quantities of supplementary supplies had to be hauled from Skagway, on the Alaskan coast, to Whitehorse, at the head of navigation on the Yukon River system.

Placed in service in 1901, the 36-inch, narrow-gauge White Pass & Yukon Railroad had undergone little development since its original construction equipment operating on the line in mid-1942 consisted of 9 locomotives, 186 revenue freight cars and 14 passenger cars, the majority of which were over 40 years old. Track had originally been laid with light 45- and 46-pound rail rolled before 1900. Like the Alaska Railroad, the WP&Y owned and operated allied facilities, including the ocean dock at Skagway and a river steamship line out of Whitehorse.

Operating with limited and antiquated equipment over a rugged route, the railroad was unable to clear cargo laid down at Skagway. By the autumn of 1942 it was fast becoming a bottleneck in the flow of supplies into western Canada. At the direction of General Somervell, who had inspected the line in August, the railroad was leased by the Army, effective October 1, 1942. By this time a railway detachment of 9 officers and 351 enlisted men had been activated and shipped from Seattle, and arrangements were being made to purchase and ship American rail equipment.

Engineer Railway Detachment 9646A arrived at Skagway in mid-September 1942 and set up headquarters. After a brief period of instruction, the detachment took over the operation and maintenance of the railroad. With the continued assistance of the civilian employees, the troops acted as mechanics, engineers, dispatchers, firemen, conductors, telegraphers, section hands, brakemen, and track-walkers. Upon the transfer of the Military Railway Services from the Engineers to the Transportation Corps in November 1942, the unit was redesignated the 770th Railway Operating Detachment, Transportation Corps.

Under military operation, the railroad had carried 14,231 tons in October, about 3,000 tons more than the previous month. It was expected that equipment scheduled for early arrival would further accelerate traffic, but severe winter weather struck the area in December, and for a three-month period high snowdrifts, ice, snowslides and sub-zero temperatures made the line's operation and maintenance a nightmare. Rotary snowplows preceded all trains, but occasionally drifts were too high to cut through and trains were isolated. Ice on the rails resulted in the frequent derailment of locomotives and cars, and when trains stopped, they froze to the tracks. Traffic slowed to a trickle, and the line was completely immobilized for 10-day periods in December and February.

While the troops were battling to keep the line in operation, plans were being made to increase the railroad's personnel and equipment. In view of increased Northwest Service Command estimates of supply requirements, an MRS survey was made in early 1943, following which the Transportation Corps undertook to provide the additional troops, rolling stock and motive power necessary to handle 1,200 tons daily by May. On April 1, the detachment was redesignated the 770th Railway Operating Battalion, with an authorized strength of 19 officers, 2 warrant officers and 708 enlisted men. Technical supervision of the railroad, previously exercised by the MRS headquarters, was transferred to the Commanding General.

As the weather improved, and additional personnel and equipment were placed in service, rail operations also improved. Traffic, virtually all northbound from Skagway to Whitehorse, climbed from 5,568 tons in February to a peak of over 40,000 tons in August. By autumn 1943 the backlog of freight at Skagway had been cleared and the railroad was hauling all tonnage offered.

During 1943 the WP&Y carried 284,532 tons, more than 10 times the traffic handled in 1939, and transported some 22,000 troops and civilian construction workers to Whitehorse. The right of way had been improved, 25 locomotives and 284 freight cars had been added to the roster, and night operations had been initiated. The entire responsibility for maintenance and operation rested with the 770th Railway Operating Battalion, assisted by some 150 civilians. To say that they performed heroic miracles would be an understatement. Authorities within the Military Railway Service agree that these men were the unsung heroes of supply and operation on the North American continent during World War II.

Railway Operations in North Africa

In the autumn of 1942 U.S. troops under Lieutenant General Dwight D. Eisenhower invaded North Africa with support from British Naval and Air units. Among the first Transportation Corps troops to be landed at Oran, Algiers and Bone, in North Africa, were detachments from Military Railway battalions, whose duties included the unloading and erecting of locomotives, the clearing of local yards, and the opening of main line traffic. When American service units landed along with the large shipments of supplies at Casablanca, they found the transportation situation well under the control of Colonel Clarence L. Burpee and Major Jesse M. McLellan, both of the Atlantic Coast Line. Railroads throughout Morocco were under French and Arabic operation, and remained so, but the splendid job done by these American railroad officers accelerated and coordinated the service to a degree of efficiency necessary to handle the enormous overload. American Military Railway units took over the operations of the principal railroads in eastern Algiers and all roads in Tunisia not occupied by the enemy. The first MRS troops to arrive were assigned the task of operating the narrow-gauge lines extending southeast from Ouled Rahmound (the junction just south of the important rail center at Constantine) through Tebessa into Tunisia. These were the most important arteries until Rommel was pushed north of Sousse.

In the North African theater, all available railway facilities had to be utilized as promptly and fully as possible. The main railway, a single-track line during most of the war, ran roughly parallel to the North African coastline, from Casablanca to Tunis via Fes, Oujda, Oran, Algiers and Constantine, a total of 1,410 miles. From Casablanca to Fes the main line was electrified; eastward of Fes it depended upon steam. Freight capacity was estimated at 240 tons of military supplies per day per train, yielding a total of 5,760 tons for 12 trains per day each way. The Military Railway Service became active in North Africa at a time when the campaign was nearing its critical stage. In order to expedite the movement of supplies and troops, the General Manager of the MRS, General Gray, assigned the bulk of the available U.S. railway units to operations in the forward area. Early in March 1943 the 703rd Railway Grand Division disembarked at Mers el Kebir. Assigned to the 703rd were the 727th Railway Operating Battalion, which had already begun operations on the overtaxed Ouled Rahmoun-

At the desert training center in California, trucks and equipment of an armored division are about to be moved to a new camp area. (10-22-42)

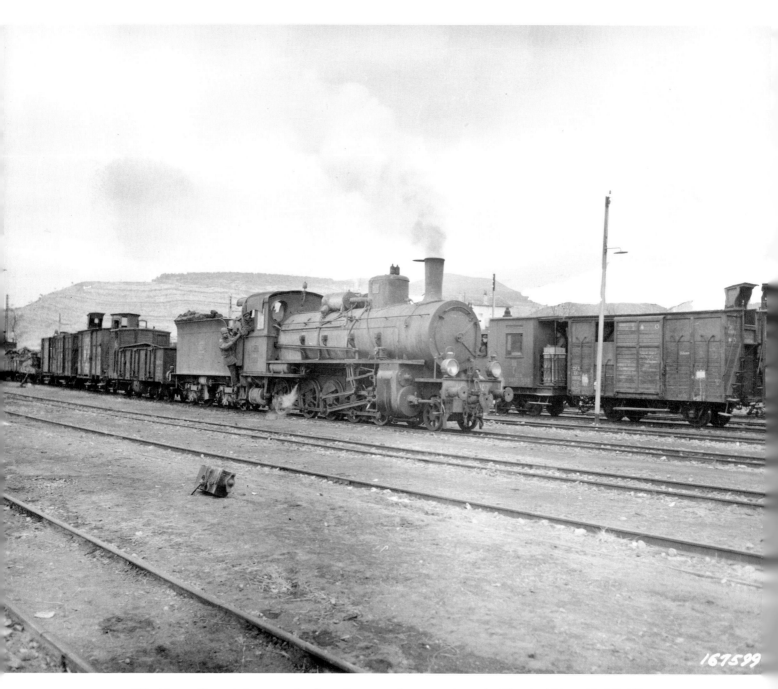

Working a French locomotive in railway yards somewhere in North Africa. (2-17-43)

Tebessa line during the previous month, and the newly arrived 713th Railway Operating Battalion, which was given jurisdiction over the lines from Beni Mansour through Constantine to Philippeville.

Stationed nearest the battlefront, the 727th operated uncomfortably close to the German troops of General Rommel. On February 14, for example, when the loss of Gafsa appeared imminent, Colonel Jack Okie, aided by a small detachment of the 727th and three trucks, attempted to evacuate highly essential railway rolling stock and war material. Four of the imperiled locomotives and 16 cars of ammunition were caught behind a blown-out bridge at Sidi Bou Baker, on the rail line to Thelepte. The detachment had just succeeded in concealing eight locomotives in a mine tunnel near Moulares and were in the process of immobilizing them by removing vital parts when the approach of an enemy tank caused Colonel Ikoe to hastily load his men and engine parts on trucks and leave for Redeyef. En route, the party was fired upon by native troops, but avoided further attack by waving a French flag. After picking up 26 French civilians and their baggage at Redcycf, the Americans set out across the desert via Tamerza to Bir el Ater, walking and pushing the trucks for several miles through deep sand. The detachment finally reached the road running north into Tebessa, arriving there on February 16 with gas tanks almost empty.

Army railroading in North Africa was done the hard way. G.I. engineers and firemen, for example, got used to standing in the cabs because French locomotives carried no seating accommodations! On various occasions, engine crews stood for as long as 30 hours on runs, without relief. In the United States, the caboose was reserved strictly for the crews; in North Africa, the caboose became a haven for deadheads, including some French soldiers, civilians and as many Arabs as could crowd in. More often than not, the Arabs brought with them a variety of livestock, such as chickens, goats and sheep. Scattered along the trackside over the breadth of North Africa were the soldiers who dispatched the trains, repaired the rolling stock when it broke down, maintained the roadbed, replaced blown-out bridges and assembled new locomotives. They lived in tents, railway stations, bomb-shattered houses, and small hotels—anything they could find with a roof over it.

The trains which came under the control of the Military Railway service rolled in a variety of equipment, ranging from the old World War I type ("40 hommes, 8 chevaux") box cars to modern steel gondolas brought from the United States. Although the main line which followed the coast was of standard gauge, the branches that went off to the south were 1-meter and 1.05-meter gauges. The locomotives ranged in type from electric and diesel-electric to steam, and in vintage from 1899 to just before the war. American locomotives were shipped in crates and assembled in the shops at the ports. Railroading in North Africa was performed by an international melange of United States, British and French military personnel, and French and Arab civilians, with troops exclusively handling movements near the front. Obviously, such railroading was rich in anecdote. One report of an engineer's experience gives an idea of the difficulties under which the trains operated:

I am taking this rattler along about 45 miles an hour when we start down a 2 percent grade. Further along we pick up 10 miles an hour. I think that'll be enough, so I whistle once for brakes. Over here we have no air, but have Arab brakemen scattered along the train with hand brakes. One whistle means brakes—most of the time, not always. This time all the brakemen were asleep.

By and by, this choo-choo is rolling along at 65 miles an hour. My fireman is sitting on the French engineer to keep him away from the throttle. He wants to reverse the thing. You can do that on a French engine, but on this Yankee engine, it would have stripped the valve gears.

You're supposed to stop at every station to get clearance for the next—not my train, for we went through four stations, and the *chefs de gare* were all out waving at us and hollering like hell for us to stop. Back in the caboose, I learned later, the lieutenant had the French conductor down in a corner and was sitting on him to keep him from jumping. Finally, we hit an up-grade and slowed down. So we went back and slapped the Arabs awake and went on, a way ahead of schedule.

Such annoyances were a lot better than coming under direct enemy fire. On February 17, 1943, when the Thelepte airfield was abandoned, a second detachment of the 727th, under 1st Lieutenant Victor E. Williams, was shot at while attempting to remove valuable rail equipment. When Rommel's forces broke through the Kasserine Pass, the battalion got ready to evacuate Tebessa itself. However, by the morning of February 25, the enemy had retreated, leaving behind numerous deadly mines and several badly damaged bridges. Railway repair and reconstruction progressed rapidly in the recaptured area, and within 15 days after the German withdrawal the line was open to Kasserine.

At the peak of activity in North Africa, Allied freight traffic, based on a total mileage of 1,905 for all sections, totaled 31,554,660 ton-miles. The end of hostilities in North Africa altered the transportation pattern of heavy movements of men and materials from west to east. Thereafter a two-way flow of traffic developed, as men and material were moved both into and out of Tunisia. The inbound traffic was largely in preparation for the projected invasion of Sicily and Italy. Already in progress, but much accelerated by the Axis surrender, the outbound movement involved mostly personnel.

One of the highest tributes to the soldier-railroaders operating in North Africa was paid by Lieutenant Colonel Ralph E. Sherer, Chief Maintenance of Way Officer, Military Railway Service, when he said:

> Upon capture of enemy-held territory, the first duty of the Military Railway Service is to make reconnaissance of rail lines and equipment, in anticipation of their immediate use to support advancing troops. The actual rehabilitation of rail lines, construction of new trackage, repairs to bridges, clearing of antipersonnel mines and enemy demolitions, ordinarily are duties of the corps of engineers. But we discovered early in the North African campaign that more often than not the engineers were too busy with combat units to assist in getting the rail lines back in operation in the shortest possible time.
>
> But what about us? Well, let's take North Africa first: We were stretched across the North coast of that continent with a rather excellent roadbed of single track; with small main terminals, inadequate and insufficient passing and operating tracks at intermediate stations; with cars that remind one of "cracker boxes"; with trains operated, not with air brake control, but by sleepy Arab brakemen; with no signals worth the name; no headlights on our engines; no modern coal and water facilities; and through many tunnels and over grades of 2½ and 3 percent. Until you all sent us some good American 2-8-0 locomotives, we had the most unbelievably inadequate and obsolete power that it has ever been a man's misfortune to have to run, or it should be said, try to run.
>
> In addition to these physical disabilities, we are confronted with an operating procedure that is as far apart from ours as is the North pole from the South. The dispatching system does not contemplate a good old American train dispatcher actually directing the movement of and ordering meets for trains, but places the whole responsibility on the "Chef de Gare" (station master) who tries to operate on a station-to-station block system for train movement. Since these operating rules will not mix any better than oil and water, we have either had to adapt ourselves to their ways, or take over the line in its entirety and operate it under standard rules and practices.
>
> But our Military Railway Service has yet to find an obstacle too difficult to surmount, if not in orthodox fashion, then by squeezing out of necessity whatever invention is required to reduce the insuperable to the negotiable.
>
> You may be certain that wherever our battle lines move, the Military Railway Service will be in the thick of things, achieving new triumphs in rail-building, maintenance, and operation. These men are good soldiers—as good soldiers as they are railroad men, and there are no better railroad men to be found.

An MRS-operated locomotive strains and chugs up a long incline toward a mountain pass near Oujda, North Africa. (5-10-43)

At the boxcar assembly line in Oran, North Africa, a chain hoist was used to turn a car underframe in the process of lowering it onto the tracks. (4-6-43)

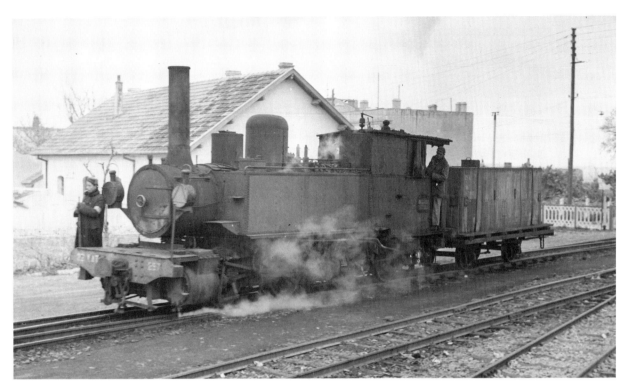

The MRS helping in the operation of a French locomotive in railway yards in North Africa. (2-17-43)

Sgt. Leslie Gross, Jerseyville, IL, and Cpl. Andrew Sajda, Gary, IN, happily guard a carload of French wine aboard a train captured at St. Leu, Algeria. (11-8-42)

Near Oujda, French Morocco, North Africa, Cpl. Rhobidien Dyal, Plant City, FL, gazes from the window of his halftrack, "Moonshine T." Seated on the flat car are Cpl. Carroll Wetski, Richmond, TX, Pfc. Charles Fisher, Mount Etna, IA, and Sgt. H.L. Smith, Conyer, GA. (5-10-43)

American diesel pulling Egyptian freight cars out of the 760th yard at Simila, Egypt. (7-2-43)

A group of locals on the platform at Rabat to welcome the first all-American train in North Africa as it arrives from Casablanca. (3-31-43)

A freight train in Algeria loaded with supplies and leaving for an unknown destination. (6-12-43)

III
War Railroading in Italy and Iran

The North African campaign to drive the Axis armies from Africa and to free the Mediterranean as a route for supplies to the Near and Far East was over. Between 1939 and 1942 Axis domination reached from Alexandria to Dakar and threatened not only Egypt, but also South America. The Allies had been forced to transport supplies around the Cape of Good Hope (6,000 miles or 50 additional days round-trip) to Alexandria for the British 8th Army, which was feverishly building up supplies to stop Rommel, and to the Persian Gulf for Russia, then desperately defending Stalingrad. Furthermore, victory in North Africa meant that the continent's ports could be used as launching points for invasion of the "soft" underside of Europe, taking advantage of the fact that with Spain neutral, and France an unwilling Axis partner, Italy could be forced out of the war. The principal objective of the Mediterranean campaign had been accomplished and approximately two million tons of essential supplies had been brought to the Allied cause via the shortened route.

The North African campaign furnished an excellent example of the value of rail transportation, or rather the difficulty of waging successful war without it. In reviewing the North African operations, the most serious faults in railway work could be listed as follows: (1) lack of knowledge of the language where the railroads were; (2) lack of motor vehicles for transportation of supervisory officers and for reconnaissance; (3) lack or slow delivery of equipment and repair parts from the United States; (4) lack of sufficient dirt-moving equipment.

The Military Railway Service was determined to learn from these lessons. Starting with the landing of the 727th Railway Operating Battalion at Licata, Sicily, on July 12, 1943, three days behind the invasion forces, railway operation was promptly restored, despite blown-up bridges and tunnels. The Allied front lines were so well supplied with munitions and rations that the Axis withdrew in short time to Messina. When Palermo was opened by the American forces on July 28, the Military Railway Service was ready to furnish rail service east to the army then fighting at Cefalù and Castelbuene along the rocky coast of Sicily. When put back to work, the Italian railway forces proved most cooperative. It was in this theater that the 727th Railway Operating Battalion was cited by the Commanding General of the 7th Army for its outstanding work.

The 703rd Railway Grand Division put an advance party ashore with the early invasion troops at Salerno, Italy. When the 727th Railway Operating Battalion came in from Sicily, the 703rd moved in reinforced strength to Naples, where it was soon joined by the 713th Railway Operating Battalion. There, the first task was to dig out and repair one track to serve the waterfront, where the engineers and the Navy had cleared enough space of sunken ships to reach the dock wall. A few cars and a nondescript steam locomotive were used to transport supplies along this track to the 5th Army near Caserta five days after they landed. The troops then turned their attention to the shambles that had been made by Allied bombing and German demolition of the waterfront, the railway yards at the Central Station and every bridge, subway, water tank, locomotive, frog and switch on the double-track main line toward Sparanise and Vairane, and on the single-track line to Benevento on the way to serve the airfield at Foggia.

Meanwhile, the Germans had invented a new instrument of destruction in Italy, a track destroyer. This was a large structural-steel hook, or bull-tongued plow, pivoted on a flat car so that its point could be dropped below the ties in the middle of the track. Pulled by three locomotives, there was sufficient power to plow up the middle of the track, breaking all the

Loaded freight cars jammed the Lolli station in Palermo, Sicily. (1-8-44)

A freight train moving onto the main line out of the Canicatti, Sicily, railroad yards. (1943)

ties. At the same time, small demolition charges were dropped on each side, to be clipped to and blow out a section of the center of each rail. Luckily, they used this machine on the double-track main line from Naples to Rome and did not have time to complete the destruction of both tracks. On this line, there was also very thorough destruction of bridges, requiring "shoo fly" diversions, with tractor-scrapers and bulldozers moving large quantities of grading materials.

Work was expedited by moving up all of the maintenance-of-way companies from the Operating Battalions in North Africa, by the use of several Army engineer units, and by the organization of Italian railway construction battalions and civilian contract gangs. Because of these forces, on January 1, 1944, the lines were open from Naples north to Vairane, to Foggia in the east, and to Bari and Tarante in the southeast. The line up the east coast along the Adriatic, behind the 8th Army, was opened from Tarante to Vaste under the direction of the British Railway Forces. Many of these lines had been used by electric locomotives, supplied in part by hydro-electric power from plants now behind the German lines. These roads had to be used by steam locomotives—the few which had escaped total destruction by the Germans. Luckily, it was possible to ship in some locomotives by ferrying them across from Sicily and routing them through Metaponta and Potenza to Naples.

Operation of the electrified lines by steam locomotives was a hazardous undertaking, since the many tunnels were unventilated. Several trainmen and 500 or more helpless passengers were asphyxiated when their train became caught in a tunnel near Potenza in March 1944—perhaps the worst railroad tragedy in history. This was certainly no fault of the Military Railway Service, since guards were never numerous enough to prevent unlawful riding on car rods and roofs. In fact, that particular train was operated by an Italian crew and no Americans were present. Since coal was a scarce article in Italy, all U.S. locomotives were equipped as oil-burners.

The brunt of railway reconstruction in the areas behind the 5th Army was borne by the A Companies and signal sections of the 713th, 715th, 719th, 727th and 759th Railway Operating Battalions, assisted by two battalions of Italian construction troops. Even when tracks and bridges were ready for service, there was the problem of providing fuel to run the trains, since Italy lacked coal reserves. In order to make the maximum use of fuel oil, General Manager Carl Gray decided in October 1943 to obtain as many diesel engines as possible and to convert U.S. and Italian coal-burning locomotives into oil-burners. By the end of February 1944, a total of 49 U.S. diesel engines had been placed in operation in Italy. Of the 14 U.S. standard 2-8-0 coal-burning locomotives received from North Africa during that month, 11 were converted into oil-burners. Sizable quantities of both coal and fuel oil had to be imported to keep the trains in operation.

The Military Railway Service accomplished considerable shop work. Two American and three British hospital trains were converted from captured equipment and used to transport patients during the winter of 1943-1944. The second American 14-car hospital train, completed on February 11, 1944, was much superior to the first, having both electric lighting and steam heat. Other jobs performed during 1944 included the construction of a nine-car "delousing" train for 5th Army troops at the front and the manufacture of replacement parts for baking equipment at the Ansio beachhead.

Important in all this work was the success of the MRS in repairing electric engines and restoring service on the electrified lines that the Germans had left behind in an utterly useless state. Diesel-electric engines were kept rolling by the machinists and electricians of the 760th Railway Diesel Shop Battalion, which began functioning at Bagnoli in late November 1943. By January 1944, Allied rail traffic in Italy had begun to mushroom. For example, lines totaling approximately 2,400 miles were then under the operations control of the MRS. Often the soldier-railroaders worked within sight of combat. During the closing months of 1943

A U.S. Army welder cutting rails which were wrecked in bombing at the Malta River bridge near Civitavecchia, Itally. (7-20-44)

the military demands for movements by rail were coordinated and the allotments of rail tonnage were decided by means of weekly rail Priority of Movements meetings attended by representatives of the Peninsular Base Section, the Advance Administrative Echelon, Allied Forces Headquarters, and the Military Railway Service.

While the MRS struggled to restore rail service and to satisfy both military and civilian demands, its operations were by no means trouble free. For example, the thick blanket of volcanic ash and cinders left by the violent eruption of Mt. Vesuvius in March 1944 halted railway traffic for nearly two days. Furthermore, German aircraft continued to strafe trains and to bomb railway facilities, striking in the Naples area as late as April 1944. As in North Africa, trains carried anti-aircraft guns and gunners.

On April 30, 1944, the MRS, under the direction of the General Manager, had the following U.S. Army military railway units stationed in Italy: two railway grand divisions, four railway operating battalions, and Company A of another; one railway shop battalion; a detachment of one railway diesel shop battalion; one provisional base depot company; a military police battalion; and a separate military police company. These units totaled 7,418 officers and enlisted men, operating some 504 locomotives, of which 296 were available and 208 were under repair. Railway cars in service numbered 18,961.

As the war in Italy drew to a close, the major emphasis of MRS activity was placed upon the reconstruction and restoration to service of the lines in the north, which were vital to the 5th Army. To the south, as the wartime urgency lessened, portions of the rail network were progressively released to the Italian State Railways. Military traffic continued heavy in 1945. In April of that year, for example, 377 military freight trains delivered 151,827 net tons from Leghorn to Pisa.

The following eyewitness account of what war railroading was like in Italy is told by Technical Sergeant Louis L. Russel, who served with the 713th Railway Operating Battalion:

On the morning of October 6, 1943, as I leaned against the rail of a transport ship, I looked upon a ghost city [probably Naples], or perhaps I should say skeleton. As Navy gunners constantly squinted at the sky, members of our railway operating battalion climbed down mesh rope ladders into armored landing barges. The harbor was full of such barges as they scooted back and forth, unloading a convoy of fighting men. The LCI on which I was riding gingerly picked its way through the many masts of sunken ships, and occasionally the bottom side of a ship would appear here and there, looking like a long slice of watermelon dropped upside down into the sea. The buildings along the wharf were still smoking and in utter wreckage. The silent city lay stretched before us, gaunt and weary.

Our battalion was finally assembled in the dock area and we marched away. In some battered warehouses at the west end of the railroad yard, we were quartered. We were dirty and tired from a seven-day trip across the Mediterranean, but there was no water for bathing. The retreating Germans, who were then only 10 miles to the north of us, had blown up the water mains. All water was hauled by tanks on trucks, even for the long strings of civilians waiting with their bottles and jugs.

Late that afternoon the men began to make a preliminary inspection of the yards. The demolition had been terrific. Charred and twisted cars were strewn around haphazardly, with lengths of rail cross ties still attached, pointing toward the sky. About 9:30 that night, while the men were restlessly settling down under the incessant booming and flashing of heavy artillery to the north, we experienced our first air raid in Italy. There were no air raid shelters nearby, so we watched through doors and the holes in the roof, while hundreds of tracer bullets streaked skyward and flak burst high above us.

The next day I accompanied some of our officers and non-coms on a tour of the yards. That was on a Wednesday. First Lieutenant R.H. Anderson, yardmaster, from Newton, Kansas, said, "I believe that we can get a train out this way by Sunday." I had my own ideas about getting trains or anything else through that mess for a month, but I asked him, "You mean Sunday after next?" I wanted to ask him: "What are you going to use for engines? Where are you going to get the cars? And after you get them, where are you going to run them?"

Damaged railroad yards in Naples, Italy, being repaired by Italian workmen under the supervision of the MRS. (12-7-43)

At Naples, Italy, finishing touches are put on the "General Gruenther Express," one of many salvaged Italian locomotives used to transport matériel to the various fronts. (11-13-43)

Four days later, on Saturday, a train was run northward for a distance of four miles. It was a test train, a wheezing, old Italian 0-6-0 class engine pushing ahead of it five cars. Conductor Woodrow Boice, Chicago, and his brakemen handled the switches gingerly on this trip, since many of them had been discovered to be mined. Four days later, six trains, averaging 450 tons each, were moved to the forward railhead. During the first week of operation 45 tonnage trains were moved over a total of 588 miles to deliver 31,839 gross tons of munitions and supplies to the front lines. Some five months later, during one week, 126 tonnage trains were operated over 2,390 miles of track to handle 75,758 gross tons.

Bear in mind that, to begin with, our shop forces of "B" Company had three beat-up Italian locomotives that the Germans had either overlooked or scorned to waste time and powder on. We found what had been two fine roundhouses a maze of debris, with all machinery cleverly damaged. Within a few days "B" Company had set up enough machinery to service eight more Italian engines which had been dug out of the wreckage. These engines were used in switching on the few tracks that had been repaired in the yard and in handling supplies from the docks to these yards.

Company "A", the maintenance-of-way forces, had pitched into the melee with even more fervor than that with which they had distinguished themselves in North Africa, where they won a Legion of Merit award for their commanding officer, then Captain and now Major Hal E. Wilson, assistant superintendent. This gang cleared away a number of tracks, and on October 10 they moved up about seven miles to the north and about an equal distance behind the retreating enemy. There, during four cold and rainy days, they cleared away damaged equipment and litter, placing and tying down 8,500 feet of rail. Moving right on the heels of the 5th Army infantry, this group of men rolled up their muddy pup tents and moved, on October 21, 10 miles further north. There, in seven days, they put into use 18,000 feet of utterly destroyed track. Putting in this amount of track included clearing away wrecked equipment, tearing out old rail, cutting and drilling rail, surfacing and tying down rail ready for use. During this time it was necessary to repair damaged bridges and construct impressive fills. They continued in this manner, working from sunup until sundown, making it possible for the vital railway supply line to keep the front lines stocked with munitions and equipment. At times they were bawled out by the artillery units for getting in their way. In short, they were living the life of combatants with little time to protect themselves while doing noncombatants' work.

Dispatching trains was quite a job. The dispatcher's biggest problem was amply summed up by Technical Sergeant Jack M. Longfellow, of Winslow, Arizona, "I know if ever I am a failure, I can blame it on failures—engine failures." In keeping his trains rolling, Dispatcher Longfellow many times sent out an engine to bring in an engine, only to have to send out another to bring them both in. It was no reflection on the shop forces. They just simply could not make something out of nothing. Those were the pioneer days of "haywire" days. It wasn't exactly baling wire, but wire did give the dispatchers many a headache. The railroad lines we had reclaimed had been converted to use as electric locomotives prior to the war. All of this overhead wire had been cut and blasted so that the right of way looked as though so much oversize confetti had been strung about. Even after hastily clearing away this entanglement, sabotage or destiny would leave more of it in the path of heavy trains. Often as not, a train would grind to a stop, securely bound and wrapped. The operator would then laconically call in to the dispatcher, "Well, we are all tied up again." Now the dispatchers handle as many as 60 trains per day with efficiency and ease.

One gang, composed of engineers, firemen, brakemen and yard clerks, made quite a name for themselves. They became known as "Sgt. Tomer's Reclamation Department." Sergeant Fred A. Tomer, of Mattoon, Illinois, was a conductor, but he took charge of the willing men and they pushed through the wreckage like a bulldozer. This gang at first cleared and placed track, then as many Italian laborers were put into the yards, Tomer wound up reclaiming serviceable cars. On looking around, he found a German wrecking crane and was soon snagging out as high as 100 cars per day from the wreckage. Another gang, under the direction of Sergeant Ralph M. Whitton, of El Paso, Texas, cleared away miles of mangled and tangled catenary wire, which was strung over and across the tracks.

The company received a letter of commendation from the Director General regarding the fine manner in which they had adapted themselves to the critical situation and performed strange work with remarkable results.

This situation soon reversed itself and the transportation company had more than it could handle. Enough engines had been put into service, counting some G.I. engines which had arrived, to require 30 switch crews and 20 road crews. This did not include yardmasters, yard clerks, switch tenders, etc., all of which were drawn from the crew roster. The crews were working furiously, never getting sufficient rest. The first sergeant stood guard, the supply sergeant went firing and the platoon sergeant went out as a conductor, all because of an acute shortage of men with heavy tonnage moving to the front. Thirty full crews from the 727th Railway Operating Battalion were attached with us to help handle the booming business. These men, veterans of the North African campaign, said that they had never been so hard pressed as they were during December and January, when we had every available man hard at the task.

Soon after the first part of 1944, a few U.S.A. diesels began to arrive, then came a number of G.I. oil-burning locomotives. Breakdowns on the road began to cease, yard facilities at intermediate points were being increased, track conditions were greatly improved, and this, with overall general improvements, resulted in a higher tonnage rate than ever being handled with more ease.

When you think or read of the 5th Army, you will be thinking and reading also of the 713th Railway Operating Battalion. We came in with them, and when the 5th is on the move again we hope to be moving with them. When I say "with" them, I mean just that. As one of our conductors Sergeant John D. Hall, Harrisburg, Pennsylvania, said, "Fellows, I almost made a terrible mistake today. We went so far up the 'boot' that I durn near turned my train over to a German yardmaster before I realized where I was."

The invasion of Italy by the Allied Forces in 1943 brought a further extension of the authority and responsibilities of Major General Carl R. Gray Jr., the Director General of the Military Railway Service. The orders governing the operation of military railways in North Africa were continued in general but were amplified on October 22, 1943, by General Orders No. 60, Allied Forces Headquarters (AFHQ). Under this directive, the Director General became responsible for the rehabilitation, technical development and operation of all Italian state and privately owned railways, except for those portions which might be returned to civilian operation under supervision of the Transportation Subcommission of the Allied Commission.

All United States Railway Service troops, the railway portion of the British Transportation Service, and Italian railway personnel and material came under the Director General's disposal and operated under his direction. General Di Raimondo and all of the Italian military railway organization were ordered to report to Gray to carry out duties assigned them. Reconstruction and operation of the Italian railways was governed by priorities established by AFHQ which was represented on the Italian mainland by the Deputy Chief Administrative Officer of the Advanced Administrative Echelon, AFHQ.

Additional British Transportation troops of both Railway Operating Groups and Railway Construction Groups were brought to Italy from Egypt with the invasion forces. Units of the Military Railway Service were transferred from North Africa to Sicily to support the U.S. 1st Army. Although the British troops supported the British 8th Army, all were under the direction of the Director General. Gray opened his first headquarters in Naples and subsequently moved it to Rome in July 1944.

Men of the 639th and 688th Machine Gun Battalions prepare to fire on an enemy reconnaissance plane over the Naples railroad yards. (12-11-43)

In Sicily, Cpl. Robert Evelyn, Redlands, CA, and Pfc. Charles Sparlins, Vancouver, WA, ride a foot-propelled railroad vehicle. (7-13-43)

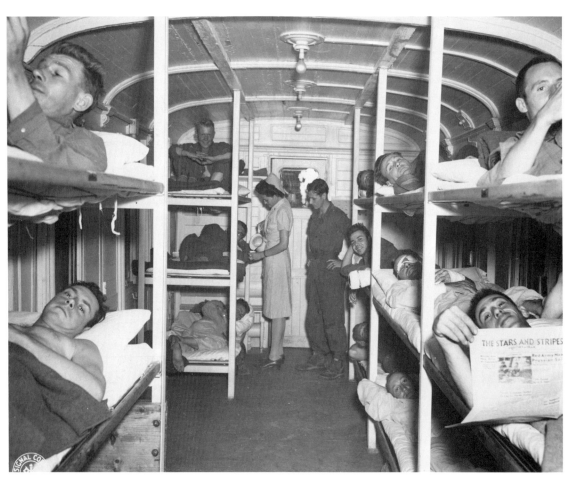

One of 13 cars of the 42nd Hospital train, the first to carry battle casualties of the northern Italian front from Rome to Naples. (7-11-44)

A coal train pulled into Cassino, Italy, on the first Naples-Rome service after the Allied occupation. (7-20-44)

Pvt. Lewis Hinaman, Bine Meadow, CN, and T/5 Lauri Arklander, Andover, OH, 36th Combat Engineers, replace a tie near Battipaglia, Italy. (9-26-43)

Pfc. Ray Penlend (Cander, NC), Pfc. Anthony Kowaliziewski (Buffalo, NY), Pvt. Jack Gimpel (Cleveland, OH), Pvt. Johnny Kilby (Danville, IL), and Sgt. Paul Miller (Butler, PA) fill craters under the tracks near Battipaglia, Italy. (9-26-43)

The 36th Combat Engineers use a crane to fill a crater before straightening the tracks near Battipaglia, Italy. (9-26-43)

S/Sgt. M.E. Smith, Jakin, GA, and Sgt. Joe Wierzba, Bruce, WI, use jacks to straighten twisted rails near Battipaglia, Italy. (9-26-43)

An American-made locomotive used by the Military Railway Service, Rome, Italy. (1-31-46)

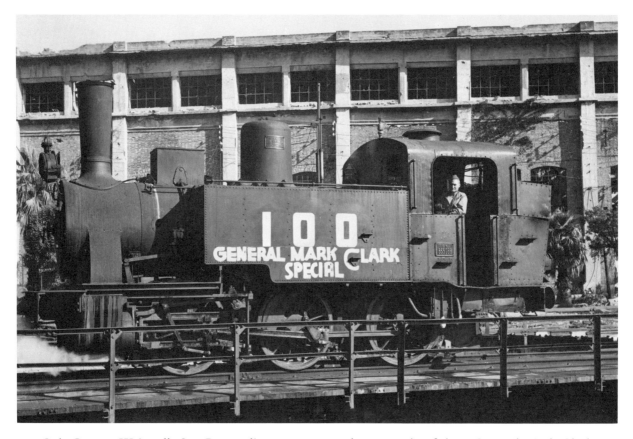

Cpl. George Weinzell, San Bernardino, CA, was at the controls of the "General Mark Clark Special" as it crossed a turntable in the Naples railroad yards. (11-13-43)

Train cars, reconstructed by the MRS, in the Naples railway yard. (12-11-43)

The first two trains to run on the repaired Naples-Rome railroad arrived in Rome simultaneously. The train on the right brought Secretary of War Henry L. Stimson. (7-20-44)

Engineers repair the railroad station in Caserta, Italy. Its rails had been blown up by the Germans at 100 foot intervals. (11-6-43)

Blocked by the bombing of railroad bridges farther north, the Germans destroyed the trucks of these coal cars by placing demolitions in the journal boxes. (6-13-44)

The Teheran railroad yard (Camp Atterbury) loaded to its capacity. (8-29-44)

American G.I.'s maneuver locomotives from barges onto the tracks at Fialiah Creek, Iran. The trains were used to haul freight over the U.S. supply line through Iran into Russia. (13-14-43)

The Military Railway Service in Iran

In January 1943 the MRS took over the operations of the Iranian State Railway from the British so that the volume of lend-lease shipments moving into Russia could be greatly increased. The obstacles faced were incredible. However, the fact that American Army railroaders had done an outstanding job was evidenced in early 1944 when 11 officers of the MRS were decorated with the Order of the Fatherland's War by none other than Joseph Stalin, ruler of all the Russias. Stalin said, "You have successfully performed great movements of arms, equipment and food in the Persian Gulf Command, thus affording great assistance to the Red Army in its struggle with the Nazi German invaders."

Before the coming of the railroad in Iran, the nation was one of the most inaccessible in the world and the isolation of its 4,000-foot plateau behind formidable mountain barriers brought into focus the need for modern transportation. The Iranian railroad was the outgrowth of one man's dreams. When Shah Reza Pahlevi ascended the Persian throne in 1925, he started almost immediately to allocate funds for a trans-Iranian railroad. Actual construction was started in 1928 and completed a decade later.

The line that the MRS took over ran north and south and was some 865 miles long. Tehran, the capital of Iran and the headquarters for the railroad, was located 289 miles south of Bandar-Shah, the northern terminal on the Caspian Sea. Leaving Bandar-Shahpour, the southern terminal, the railroad crossed the lowlands for 70 miles to a point where a 3,000-foot bridge carried the railroad across the Karun River into Ahwaz, the headquarters of the southern MRS division of the railroad, in the head of Khuzestan. During World War II, Ahwaz was small, being inhabited mostly by railroad employees and a few thousand natives. In the summer, all activity ceased between 11 a.m. and 4 p.m. each day due to the intense heat, with high temperatures ranging between 115 and 130 degrees.

During the autumn of 1942 the British constructed a new line south for 75 miles from Ahwaz to Khorramshahr, a new port on the Shatt-al-Arab River near the biblical Garden of Eden. North from Ahwaz, the railroad continued through the desert for 100 miles, then entered the foothills and started climbing into the wild Zagros Mountains, inhabited by the Lur tribes. There, the railroad wound through 126 tunnels, the longest of which was 1½ miles long. During the summer these canyons became roaring furnaces, since there was no wind and the rocks held the heat. At certain points the railroad climbed to an altitude of over 7,270 feet, then crossed undulating plateaus. Most of the grade was 2.8 percent, and in one spot the track was badly snarled with six bridges and four tunnels within a distance of less than 900 feet.

The Iranian State Railway was a single-track, standard-gauge railroad which cost $125 million. The maximum curvature was 8 degrees 20 minutes. In the south, much of the grade was 1.5 percent, while north of Tehran, the maximum grade was 2.9 percent. The rail weighed 67 pounds per yard and was 41 feet long. There were 17 ties per rail in tangent track and 19 ties in curves. All main track was tie-plated. The track was ballasted to a depth of 12 inches with coarse hand-broken rock or pit-run gravel. Ballast was provided by local contractors along the line, and it was hauled to the track by donkeys. The cost in 1943 was $3.50 per cubic yard. There were no rail anchors on the railroad. Six-hole angle bars were used and slot-spiked. Screw spikes were standard over the entire railroad, as these had a tendency to help prevent the rails from creeping. Also, rail anchors were ordered from the United States. In the original construction, rail had been provided by Russian, German and American firms. The rail was extremely soft and most of the difficulty experienced was due to split heads in the Russian and German rail. By late 1943 no fissures had developed in any of the rail (this was due in part to the light tonnage handled before that date).

There were over 3,000 bridges on the Iranian railroad, including several of the steel-girder type. Some were over 400 feet long and 100 feet high. Of course, there were practically no road crossings.

Travel over the railroad during the first few months after the American soldier-railroaders took over was extremely difficult. There were no camps, hotels, or even places to secure food. None of the water was safe for drinking. It was necessary for Americans, traveling either by train or on a track car, to carry a bedroll, food and water, and to simply sleep where nightfall caught them.

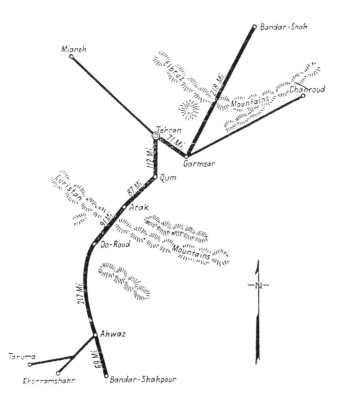

The lines of the Iranian State Railways. The main line between Bandar-Shahpour and Bandar-Shah is being operated by military personnel.

Sgt. Louis Palandrani, Dennison, OH, formerly of the Pennsylvania Railroad, was assistant supervisor for track inspection for a division of the Iranian Railroad operated by the MRS. (1944)

A Russian guard talking with the American crew of a train just prior to its departure from the Teheran yards. (4-17-44)

Mountain lions, eagles, bears, foxes, jackals, wild boars, mountain goats, sheep and gazelle were not uncommon sights along the route. Natives occasionally took pot shots at passing trains, and at night it was safer to ride with window shades drawn. From the beginning it was apparent that the first problem facing the Military Railway Service was that of securing an adequate water supply. Water in Iran came from wells, springs and streams. Pumps had to be installed and other sources tapped. At one spot, water was pumped 25 miles from a river to the point where it was needed.

When the British first came to Tehran in 1942, they found a few old Krupp engines and some 20-ton cars. Most of the cars were hand-braked, with no air. This condition was improved by securing automatic-braked cars and new locomotives from the United States. Later the MRS added additional air-braked cars and a number of 1,000-horsepower diesel engines. There were no automatic couplers on the railroad, as all equipment had screw couplings. Americans still found it hard to watch a switchman stand in the middle of the track to make a coupling. The main locomotive and car repair shops were located in Tehran and were of good fireproof construction, and well equipped with modern tools and machinery. (Much of this machinery was added after the Americans took over the railroad.) The engine terminal houses were known as "running sheds," being rectangular in design, with 6 to 12 stalls in each building. All terminals had turntables, and at most of these stations there were also wyes.

According to Lieutenant Colonel Charles T. Warren in a letter to *Railway Age* dated July 22, 1944:

The daily mail train, which originally took 30 hours and has now been cut to 25 hours for the run from Ahwaz to Tehran, is a carnival for anyone riding it the first time.

There are first, second, and third class coaches. The first and second class coaches are compartments seating eight in the day-time and providing four berths at night. The third class cars are little better than box cars with hard benches. The first class fare from Tehran to Ahwaz (495 miles) is $18. Leaving the terminal, all the relatives come down to see the departing passengers, and there is much confusion. A sharp eye must be kept on your baggage throughout the trip to prevent theft. Passengers, particularly in third class cars, get on the train with everything imaginable—chickens, ducks, goats, sheep; and the most important thing is their samovar for making tea. The cars swarm with flies and the odors are not too pleasant. At every station swarms of passengers get off to wash, get drinking water, or confer with friends; many get off to say their frequent prayers.

In the first and second class coaches are officers and soldiers from the many Allied countries— Persian, Indian, Russian, British, Polish, American, and sometimes an occasional Free-French soldier. Of course, there are the ever-present Persian police in uniform at all stations. The crowd is good natured and the soldiers of the many countries exchange views (where language and interpreters permit), swap food, drinks, reading material, etc. The trip is long, tiresome, and dirty.

One of the great difficulties in the operation of a railroad in a foreign country is the language confusion. There are a surprising number of people here, however, who speak English. This is due in great part to an American mission school which has operated in several cities in Persia for a great many years. Also, with the help of interpreters and the sign language, we have done surprisingly well. In the first few months of operation, anyone traveling over the railroad on business always took an interpreter. Now interpreters are seldom used, except in the offices. Quite a number of the illiterate coolie foremen have grasped enough English to understand what is wanted on the job and many of our soldiers, in daily contact with Iranians, speak passable Persian.

We have done things and seen practices that would not be considered good railroading back home, but when one is 10,000 miles from his base of supply, improvising becomes second nature.

We have had our problems but all the officers and men in the Transportation Corps' Military Railway Service have seen the tonnage move to Russia, so we know that our methods have got results. No one department or individual was responsible for this, but rather the combined efforts of all.

The transfer table behind the running shed at Camp Atterbury, Teheran, Iran. (1-8-45)

This locomotive was being repaired in the heavy machine shop of the Iranian State Railway. (9-30-45)

A railcycle being used
at Kuh Pank, Iran.
(11-8-43)

Diesel locomotive maintenance at the Sultanabad, Iran, shops. (4-6-44)

Engine on barge, Failiyah Creek. May 1945.

The MRS operated this train loaded with materiel on the Iranian railroad between the Persian Gulf and northern supply depots, where the Russians took over. (1944)

An American-built locomotive is moved on a flat car because the track gauge of Russian railroads is wider than that in the U.S.

Rails for the Invasion of Europe

With victories and success assured in both Italy and Iran, the Military Railway Service turned its full attention to the forthcoming invasion of Europe. Of major importance was railway transportation in Britain.

When Britain entered the war in 1939, the railways had 19,463 locomotives, 1,241,711 freight cars, and 45,838 passenger cars with a total seating capacity of 2,655,000. The total route mileage was 19,272 miles, practically all of which was laid with standard-gauge track. Judged by American standards, the number of units of equipment was large in relation to the mileage, but the capacity per unit was small. The British freight car, or "goods wagon," might move an average of only five tons, as compared with an average of 40 tons carried in an American box car. Much smaller than its American counterpart, the British passenger car was designed to effect ready discharge of passengers from many compartments and at numerous stops. One couldn't help but be impressed with the heavy movement of passenger trains, as frequent and as crowded as those of the New York City subway.

But the railroads early on had felt the impact of war, and from September 1, 1939, they found themselves under wartime controls. Because of the emergency, all freight cars were pooled, traffic was regulated on a priority basis, and passenger movements were curtailed. When American troops first began to debark, the British railways were already suffering from at least three serious handicaps: a critical shortage of manpower arising from the diversion of railway employees to wartime assignments; a sharp reduction in railway equipment because of overseas requirements, the losses of the British Expeditionary Forces in France after Dunkerque, abnormal wear and tear resulting from unusually heavy domestic traffic, and restricted new production, especially of locomotives; and a limited capacity to move tanks, other armored vehicles, and bulky Engineer and Air Force items, attributable in part to small cars and also to clearance restrictions such as those imposed by tunnels.

Early in 1944 the headquarters of the Military Railway Service was moved from London to Southampton in preparation for the forthcoming invasion of Normandy. Fairly compact office space and a sufficient number of billets were obtained in and near the city, including the Blighmont Barracks, a wing of the Civic Center, a school and two hotels. The MRS wanted to be near the action, and Southampton obviously had the greatest responsibility in the fast-approaching invasion. Nearby were 1,792,512 U.S. Army troops and 15,573,699 measurement tons of cargo.

Prior to D-Day, thousands of railway operating and shop battalion personnel converged at Southampton to initiate the first step in the forming of a well-balanced Army railway service capable of overcoming any obstacle which might block railway supply lines to the armies in the field. The units were manned with soldier-railroaders who had practical experience in North Africa, Sicily, Italy, Iran, and areas in Alaska and the Pacific. Training for the operation of French railroads began the moment the American soldier-railroaders set foot on English soil. In the English shops, the G.I.'s soon amassed records of production and assembly which astounded the British. Prefabricated cars rolled off the assembly lines in unheard of numbers, and American locomotives were conditioned and soon running over English rails, hauling supplies and troops to the ports and marshalling areas.

Eleven days after the Allies stormed ashore on the beaches of Normandy, a small detachment of the Second Military Railway Service under Brigadier General Clarence L. Burpee established a foothold on the high ground above the blood-soaked Utah Beach. Burpee's tiny band faced heavy bombing and strafing by the Germans. Armed with only light weapons and a handful of ammunition, as well as a jeep equipped with demountable flanged railroad wheels, the party had a specific mission: to analyze the railroad facilities on the beachhead, estimate damage to rails and yards, and locate all available locomotive power. Lines were surveyed all the way up the Normandy peninsula to Cherbourg. On D plus 26, the headquarters unit of the Second Military Railway Service took over operation of existing trackage in the Cherbourg yards. French engine crews helped the Americans move equipment and cars while volunteer railroad workers aided in the repair of roundhouses, shop buildings, engines and rolling stock.

Under supervision of the Railway Service, Engineer Corps troops worked energetically to repair the railway line from Cherbourg to Carentan. The 729th Railway Operating Battalion followed close on the heels of the advance party and relieved them of the burden of operating the Cherbourg terminals. The first passenger train was operated by personnel of the 729th and pulled out of Cherbourg for Carentan 16 days after the official capture of the Channel port. Things were not easy for the G.I. trainmen during their first operating experience under fire, but there was so much to do to keep supplies rolling that they had little time to worry about nightly bombing and strafing attacks by the Germans. Much of the train operation was done at night over tracks hastily reconstructed by the Engineer Corps, working in close cooperation with the Railway Service. The 728th Railway Operating Battalion and the 757th Railway Shop Battalion, together with the 707th Railway Grand Division, arrived in France shortly after the 729th, to form the nucleus of the force of 17,000 officers and enlisted men serving in railway units in France and Italy.

According to a *Railway Age* article covering the accounts of the MRS in France, a number of problems faced the Americans when they took over the French National Railway System. Unlike the first great war, when the French hauled American supplies for over a year and a half after the U.S. entered the conflict, in WWII the U.S. Army was well prepared to handle its own supply trains and traffic. But the problem of an adequate system of railway lines from the supply dumps and ports to the front lines was of the greatest importance. All yards were so badly damaged that they appeared to be hopelessly beyond repair. Long stretches of roadway had been ripped and torn by aerial bombardment, mines and other demolitions. Maintenance-of-way companies worked many sleepless days and nights without much in the way of power equipment to help clear the rails. With the aid of the Engineer Corps the G.I. trackmen moved out of the yards everything that could roll.

That situation was prevalent right up to the gates of Paris. Beyond the French capital, rail facilities had been spared the death blows of both the Germans and the Allies. The drive gained momentum and the railway units were kept continually on the move to keep pace with the armies they were to supply. Maintenance-of-way and operating crews lived on trains and made repairs from well-equipped shops on wheels. The railroads of France were a spiderweb of innumerable routes, and plans had to be drawn up showing the shortest and best through routes, and those requiring the least amount of repair. But when the drive started moving swiftly, operating crews called upon their own nerve and intuition to get their trains through.

Unlike the First World War, American soldier-railroaders in WWII found large quantities of railway equipment to work with. Of course, the Germans had taken most of the first-class power and rolling stock back to Germany, but they had also brought into France a great deal of fine equipment to bolster the overworked French power. Much of this was left behind and was being used by the Allied armies. French power which had been shot up was quickly repaired by shop battalions. Many ancient locomotives were found in the yards and put to immediate work. A number of American locomotives given to the French during the First World War were drafted into service. By the middle of December 1944 the Military Railway Service had many American steam and diesel locomotives available for use in France. There were also many cars of all types. American troops operated 12 mobile workshops, seventeen

Members of the 729th Railway Operating Battalion use a French engine to shunt rolling stock on repaired tracks of the devastated Cherbourg yards. (7-24-44)

Locomotives, tank cars and other necessary units of railroad equipment were stored in huge quantities in the 756th Railway Shop Battalion, Penrhos Junction, Caerphilly, Wales, perparatory to the invasion of Europe. (1944)

20-ton Brownhoise cranes, 22 wrecking trains, 7 wrecking cranes, two 25-ton locomotive cranes, and 31 hospital trains. Captured equipment, which included that of French, German, Austrian, Belgian and Italian origin was repaired and placed into service, totaling 402 locomotives and 29,300 cars of various types.

An interesting aspect of the role played by the MRS in France deals with the French underground efforts. The railways of France normally operated a total of 26,417 miles and were formerly owned and operated by seven great systems, two of which had been state-owned. On January 1, 1938, all the lines were merged into one French National Railway System, the Société Nationale des Chemins de Fer Français. In prewar days, through trains were operated from France to Belgium, Holland, Germany, Poland, Austria, Hungary, Romania, Yugoslavia, Bulgaria, Greece, Italy, Spain and Portugal. Through such a network the Germans were able to draw supplies from their Axis partners, as well as from occupied countries. This capability had given Hitler a decided advantage in the early years of the war. But the Germans soon lost their initial advantage. For one thing, they moved French operating crews from familiar territory into territory completely foreign to them. This placed a hardship on employees because their ration tickets were good only in their particular city or town and they were not allowed to purchase food in other sections. As a result, the crews lived almost entirely on rations which they carried with them when they left their home stations. Soon their efficiency was cut down by hunger. This small example is indicative of how the German conquest of Europe was mismanaged.

But more important were the heroic achievements of the French underground. Early in the war, the activities of the saboteurs were limited because of strict surveillance by Nazi patrols, but sand somehow appeared in lubricating oils and greases, which in turn found their way into the pistons and valves of locomotives and the journals, brakes and axles of engines and cars. Debris in the form of scraps of metal, pieces of wood and many other articles were found in the boilers and fireboxes of locomotives, causing much damage and often putting equipment out of service.

The underground did not limit its activities to the destruction of equipment, but mined and blasted small bridges and tunnels. Fortunately neither the Germans nor the French did substantial damage to larger structures. But U.S. Army bombers knocked out the large railway bridge at Orléans, creating a tie-up at that important southern junction point. French workers subsequently rebuilt the bridge using American materials, and equipment and trucks on loan from the Transportation Corps.

The Germans planned troop movement by divisions, which required considerable rolling stock. When these formations pulled up on a siding, French saboteurs would blast to the front and rear of the trains, isolating the troops. This activity not only delayed German reinforcements, but saved much valuable railway equipment for future Allied use.

At the main-line station of Vire during the early days of the drive to Paris, several trains loaded with German troops were tied up in the yards. The U.S. Army Air Force had the railway center on schedule for pinpoint bombing. Bombs were to be dropped in front of and behind the trains, blasting the track and disrupting any movement. But the French stationmaster knew there was an ammunition train on another siding directly beside the troop train. He got word through to the Americans, and the bombers scored direct hits on the ammunition train. Fifteen hundred Germans were killed in that single incident. The action also caused much damage to station buildings and prevented the movement by the Germans of any of the rolling stock from the yards. (This story was made into the film *The Train*, starring Burt Lancaster, Paul Scofield, Alan Delon, and others.)

After France was occupied by the Allies, French railway gangs emerged from hiding and enthusiastically cooperated with the Military Railway Service in clearing wreckage from yards and right of ways. Within weeks, the rails of France felt the roar of locomotives. Wounded

American soldiers will always owe a debt of gratitude to the French railroaders who teamed with G.I. crews to establish a fast, comfortable route to Cherbourg, where the wounded were placed on hospital ships for transfer to England and the United States. From Paris to Versailles the trains were handled by Americans, then French crews tied on their power and took over the long run from Versailles to Folligny, with American crews again taking over for the home stretch run to Cherbourg.

The following article, "Trucks and Trains in Battle—The Story of the Transportation Corps in France," by Private Irwin Ross, is presented in its entirety. Private Ross was attached to the Office of the Chief of Transportation, European Theater of Operations, and wrote a vivid and dramatic account of the transportation problems which were overcome by America's fighting soldier-railroaders and truckers. The article appeared in the January 1945 issue of *Harper's* magazine, whose publishers have generously consented to its reproduction in this book.

TRUCKS AND TRAINS IN BATTLE

The Story of the Transportation Corps in France

IRWIN ROSS

At midnight the train was completely loaded. Food, boxes of ammunition, gasoline, engineering equipment. The five-man crew was routed out of its pup tents. The engineer and fireman took their places in the cab, the flagman, brakeman, and conductor mounted the boxcars. The company commander pushed a case of K-rations into the cab.

"Where we off to?" the engineer asked. He was still sleepy.

"Never mind," the CO said. "Just keep going till someone stops you." He had only the vaguest idea where they were going. Somewhere up front, that was all.

Eighty-six hours later they were finally stopped, at a forward dump a few miles behind the armies. It had been a sleepless, harrowing trip. They had driven through the blackout without headlights, never knowing what loomed round the next bend. Tracks sagged dangerously when the cars passed over newly filled-in bomb craters. Snipers fired at them as they entered a tunnel. Planes strafed them. Three times they were halted by trains stalled ahead of them. Twice they stopped for lack of coal, and once for water. For fuel, they chopped up cross-ties found along the track, and for water, pressed a civilian fire pump into service.

This train ride through France epitomizes the story of military transportation in Europe. Operations in rear areas are better organized, but up forward improvisation to meet the hazards and vicissitudes of combat remains the invariable rule. It could hardly be otherwise, for from the morning of June 6th onward, the Transportation Corps in the European Theater, commanded by Major General Frank S. Ross, has been saddled with a transport job that in size and intricacy has no parallel in military history.

It is a truism that supply lines are the lifeblood of an army, and supply lines, pre-eminently, mean transportation fully as much as matériel. You must have the stuff, but you've got to move it before it does any good. Long before D-day, the Germans were probably reconciled to a landing. But they banked on the assumption that at every stage of the campaign our supplies would lag behind the forward thrust of our troops, and that in the pauses for consolidation they would have time to regroup their forces, contain our advances, and move to the counterattack.

Supply became the key to victory. If we won the "Battle of the Build-up" on the Normandy beaches and if, later, we kept the armies supplied as they advanced, we could win the war. It is noteworthy that once our initial breakthrough occurred, the only points the Germans favored with bitter-end defense were the

Hospital trains in Paris ready to leave for the front. (1-24-45)

A successful experiment by Royal Engineers proved that tracks could be laid and rail stock loaded and transported aboard a tank landing craft. (9-7-43)

ports—Brest, St. Malo, Calais, St. Nazaire, Le Havre. Their logic was incontestable: stopping the flow of supplies would stall our armies. But we were able to manage without these harbors, thanks to the fabulous artificial ports which were towed over from England to the Normandy beachheads. In the first hundred days of the invasion a million tons of supplies and a hundred thousand vehicles were unloaded in Normandy.

Once the stuff was safely ashore, the ports and beaches had to be cleared. The supplies had to roll, and now the burden was tossed to the railroads and the trucks. Transportation Corps truckers and railroaders were plagued by demolished roads and bridges, inadequate communications, combat hazards that posed a host of operational problems—above all, they were prey to the capricious turns of battle and the unpredictable requisitions of field commanders.

II

BEACHHEAD operations exemplified improvisation on the grand scale. On the first day they arrived, June 8th, the TC men helped the Engineers clear the beach of wrecked landing craft and vehicles—they worked all day, under enemy fire from the top of the cliff. They swept the sands for mines. The TC men hadn't been trained for the job, but the Engineers lacked enough sappers. Somehow they managed to clear their working space, de-mine it, get operations started.

Small craft, barges, DUKW's (amphibious 2½-ton trucks) beached the cargo; then it was transferred to trucks, the trucks dispatched to dumps—and always there was the job of untangling endless traffic snarls, keeping things moving, keeping the cargo from piling up in unmanageable heaps on the sands.

The beaches were our greatest gamble, and sometimes our margin of safety narrowed almost to the vanishing point. DUKW's were sunk by striking submerged objects or mines. It was difficult to locate ships at night. Orders were frequently issued to go out and unload any vessel standing close by. Truck drivers had their problems: roads too narrow for

safety in the blackout, delays at the dumps because of shortages of personnel and equipment. And then, on June 20th, a storm of hurricane dimensions broke, imperiling the entire operation. One of the artificial ports was largely destroyed. All work had to stop for three days, and once the storm was over, the men again had to clear the beach of wrecked landing craft, barges, and cargo. But between June 6th and June 27th thousands of tons of cargo were unloaded, and the supply battle of the beaches was won. On June 27th, Cherbourg was taken.

The capture of Cherbourg had stood first on our list of objectives, but the Germans' stubborn defense had delayed us many days. When we did take it, we couldn't put it into immediate operation. The Germans had demolished all port facilities. First the waters had to be cleared of mines, the wrecks of sunken vessels removed, wharves repaired. But Cherbourg presented additional problems: its normal cargo capacity had to be steeply raised, for it had always been primarily a passenger rather than a cargo port. New wharves and railroad spurs were built, but in addition beach operations had to be duplicated—unloading onto barges and DUKW's, towing the barges in to shore. After the port was open for traffic, tonnage figures mounted week by week. By mid-October the other major Channel ports had been captured, but they were not yet operating to any appreciable extent.

III

GETTING the supplies across the Channel, safely berthed in port, unloaded, was only a beginning. They still had to move. The armies needed three staples above all else—ammunition, food, POL (petrol, oil, lubricants). Supply lines were relatively easy to maintain when the troops were bottled up in Normandy. The hauls were short, and the trucks could easily handle them.

While the field commanders fumed and fretted during the Normandy deadlock, the supply men enjoyed a welcome breather. They had plenty of time to accumulate huge concentrations of stocks. They won the Battle of the Build-up quite handsomely. But when the breakthrough came, on July 25th, it pushed forward so rapidly that all our supply plans had to be discarded and new ones improvised. It had been planned to "phase" supply dumps across France as the armies gradually progressed—that is to say, to build up sizable dumps behind the armies every time the troops scored a sufficiently sizable advance, in order to provision them for the next jump forward. The locations of the prospective dumps were carefully predetermined. But things didn't work out that way at all.

There was no time to build up great piles of matériel just behind the lines, for as the armies advanced a forward dump today was a deserted cow pasture tomorrow. Supply depots had to remain where they were, near the Normandy beaches and Cherbourg, and the transport line had to stretch farther and farther, but not thinner; if anything, the elastic transport line had to grow in girth as it was pulled out in length.

The railroads couldn't carry the burden —not yet. Thousands of miles of roadbed had to be repaired, damaged rolling stock put back in working order, new equipment mounted on rails. It all takes time. You can't improvise a railroad by waving a magic wand over a drawing board.

But you can improvise a truckline almost that quickly. Over the long hauls, trucks can't carry as much tonnage as rails, but they're the most flexible mode of transport. Except for airplanes, of course, and airplanes could never carry more than a fraction of the high-priority supplies needed by the armies in France.

There's nothing to loading up a truck, handing the driver a strip map, and flagging him down the road. During the first weeks of invasion, truck runs got under way in this slapdash manner. But as the theorists of the Transportation Corps' Motor Transport Brigade knew all along, trucking and railroad logistics are equally complicated. A host of problems arise. Road repairs have to be co-ordinated with convoy schedules. Otherwise trucks jam up behind the bulldozers. Preventative maintenance has to be kept up on vehicles —the price of neglect is constant breakdowns. And yet trucks must continually

be on the move, leaving little time for maintenance. This brings in another element—ordnance outfits, which must be readily available for emergency repairs. Delays stall trucks for hours and days.

Communication is a constant problem. The dumps have to be told when trucks are to arrive and what they are carrying, in order to have men and equipment on hand to unload and store the stuff. Fully as important is the matter of traffic engineering: routes must be clearly marked, road rules enforced—otherwise trucks get lost, traffic clots up. A half-dozen different operations have to mesh closely if a sixteen-truck convoy is to move three hundred miles to its destination, unload without delay, and get back quickly.

IN THE first few weeks after the Normandy breakthrough, it was impossible to improvise a trucking system fast enough. Road jams were chronic, vehicles broke down and never arrived, lost drivers wandered dazedly over the countryside. Convoys kept getting kidnapped. Looking for forward dumps, unsure of their directions, drivers were easy bait for outfits in dire need of supplies. It was a simple business to direct a convoy to the wrong dump, have it unload, and send it on its way little the wiser. The armies got their supplies, but the waste effort was frightening.

The problem rapidly came to a head as Patton raced across France. Patton used his supply trucks as troop transports, in order to keep the infantry moving up behind the tanks. This threw the entire supply burden on the Transportation Corps. A thorough revision of the trucking system was called for.

The answer was the Red Ball Express, born on August 24th.

A two-road highway network, stretching over northern France, was commandeered. Traffic ran one way on each road—convoys moved from Normandy to the front on one road, returned on the other. In the forward areas the highway branched out, one route serving the First Army, the other the Third. It was a terrific haul—up to a thousand miles round trip when the troops reached the German border—the biggest trucking operation in military history, "four times as long as the Burma Road," the Red Ball people boast.

Red Ball itself is an old civilian railroad term, denoting priority shipments. Overnight the round red daub appeared on thousands of trucks, trailers, tank cars, wreckers, jeeps. Each vehicle had two drivers assigned to it. Sixty per cent of the men were Negroes.

Red Ball immediately instituted a standardized procedure for road operations, and vigorously enforced it. All trucks moved in convoy, each convoy commanded by an officer in a jeep following along in the rear—to watch out for stragglers. The trucks were spaced out at regular intervals, kept down to a speed of twenty-five miles an hour. This made for a steady, uninterrupted pace—and constant movement. Two MP battalions controlled traffic. Every couple of hours the convoys would stop for a ten-minute break, and if the men were lucky they would get doughnuts and coffee from a mobile Red Cross unit. Coffee was vital, for the drivers averaged twenty hours at the wheel, and without it they would doze off, start weaving back and forth—and crack up.

Midway between the dumps and the front was a huge bivouac area, covering several dozen square miles. A driver would bring his vehicle in from the dump, turn it over to his relief man, who would take it up forward. When the truck returned from the front, the first man would take over again for the trip back to the dump.

To keep the express line running in high gear, every technical contingency was provided for, every detail in the complicated logistical framework synchronized. Two Engineer regiments worked around the clock repairing roads and bridges. Repairs were carried on in close co-ordination with traffic control headquarters, to allow sufficient time between the passing of convoys. Red Ball ordnance crews, on the lookout for distressed vehicles, were on constant patrol. Repair shops and wreckers—huge steel cranes on wheels, to tow vehicles unable to move under their own power—were scattered up and down the road. The patrols carried a large assortment of tools and spare parts, but if a vehicle could not be repaired within a few hours the driver would be issued a new truck. Engine trouble was the most common complaint—the motors had to take terrific punishment because of the lengthy hauls and scanty time for maintenance. Communication along the thousand-mile route was largely by means of radio—high-powered transmitters mounted in 2½-ton trucks. When a convoy left the dump, a message would go out to all stations along the route, giving details as to cargo, destination, and handling. Jeep couriers were also used.

Red Ball operations were planned down to the last detail, but combat has a way of disrupting even the most farsighted schedules. A few drivers got wounded, and the bivouac area had a chronic shortage of relief men to furnish the trucks which pulled in. Sometimes the same drivers had to make the entire trip to the front, keep going for three days with only as much sleep as they could catch during ten-minute breaks or while the trucks were being unloaded at their destination.

ANYTHING can happen while armies are on the move. A convoy of seven trucks picked up some engineering equipment. They were told to report to Chartres, to unload at the Engineer depot. They found the depot had moved, and were sent to find it—to Auneau, then to Puisseaux. Once there, they discovered that the depot had pushed on again—off they went to a town 150 miles away, doggedly determined to get rid of their load. Finally they made it, unloaded the stuff, filled up with gas from a German tank car while listening to the sounds of the battle a mile away, and, as they departed a half-hour later, watched the German prisoners straggle by. They got back to their starting point eight days after venturing forth.

Drivers carried their rifles in their cabs, and frequently had to use them. Speeding through the center of Mortain, four trucks, manned by Negro drivers, were machine-gunned by ambushed Germans. The drivers fired back. One driver killed, one truck lost. Three gas trucks were strafed and bombed while unloading their tanks at a truckhead at St. Martin de Mandel. A convoy of thirteen gasoline

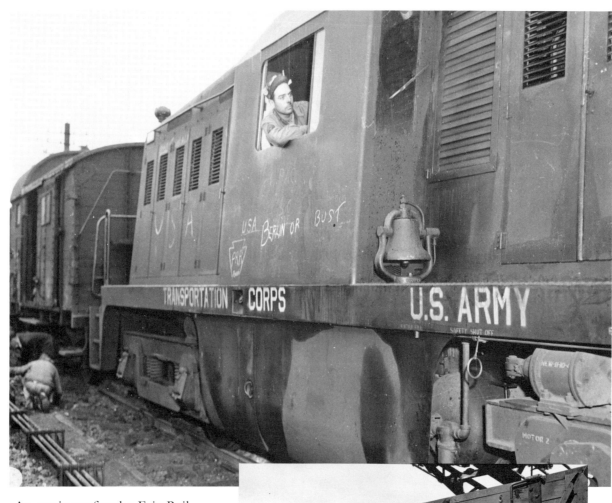

An engineer for the Erie Railroad before the war, T/4 Felton F. Cassel of Marion, OH, is at the throttle of this G.I. Supply train somewhere in France. (10-9-44)

Still showing German markings, the waybills of this captured wagon are checked somewhere in France by Pvt. Truman H. O'Neill of Birmingham, AL. (10-9-44)

At the 62nd Quartermaster Base Depot, Verdun, France, workers load B rations from trucks into freight cars. (12-3-44)

In Nevers, France, local workers clear wreckage using a locomotive that has escaped serious damage. (9-20-44)

tankers had to get through Coutances to reach Patton's army. The town had been bombed into rubble and was afire. The trucks dashed through the streets, under a blanket of shooting flames, heedless of the danger—though a stray spark igniting the fumes could have blown up the whole convoy. Patton got his gasoline.

IV

WHILE the trucks kept the armies supplied, the railroads had time to organize their forces. Railway operations in the European Theater are the responsibility of the Second Military Railway Service, commanded by Brigadier General Clarence L. Burpee. He directs twelve thousand officers and enlisted men, most of whom worked for railroads in civilian life.

The first scheduled train run, between Cherbourg and Carentan, took place on July 11th, but the first three months of operations were essentially preparatory. By mid-September thousands of miles of single- and double-track line were in shape for traffic, and tonnage figures began to zoom. Only 137,189 tons had been hauled in the first three months; by the end of September the lines were carrying an average of 10,000 tons a day—300,-000 tons a month. The rails were now doing more than Red Ball, with its 6,000 tons a day.

An elaborate organizing job faced Army railroaders when they reached the Continent. First, tracks, signal houses, marshaling and storage yards all had to be repaired before any operations could start. The Folligny yard in Normandy was a good example of conditions generally. For two years Allied bombers had smashed at the yard, raising havoc with German supply movements. Several times the Germans had repaired the damage, only to have it renewed. When the Army railroaders arrived, the yard was a nightmare of gutted cars, steel rods twisted in a hundred bizarre shapes, deep bomb craters so numerous that one merged into the other. All the railroad buildings, and most of the town, had been pounded into rubble. Parts of two buildings were left standing, and in these barren

hulks the railroad battalion that was to operate the line from Folligny to Le Mans set up shop. But before they could get to work they faced a massive job of grave-digging. The Engineers, busy repairing the yard, kept scooping up the bodies of dead German soldiers who had been buried after bombings. They had apparently been dumped into bomb craters, the earth tossed back over them, and in some cases the railroad track rebuilt over the common graves. Our men dug out all the corpses, reburied them, and then set about repairing the yard.

Since operations began on the Continent, the Corps of Engineers has rebuilt over 1,500 miles of track, erected a hundred bridges, set up marshaling yards, repaired water lines and coaling facilities. It has spanned the Seine, the Vire, the Oise rivers. One bridge was originally destroyed by our bombers, rebuilt by the Germans, demolished again by the RAF, and finally rebuilt by the Engineers.

Although the Germans had damaged a good deal of their rolling stock, much of it was salvageable. Captured railway cars were of French, Belgian, German, Czech, Rumanian, Polish make. Many of them had been damaged by bombing and shell-fire, but we put them to use. In the case of badly shattered gondolas, for instance, the sides were cut out, making them flatcars. Twelve locomotives captured in Cherbourg had been shipped to the Continent by the U. S. Army during the last war, later turned over to the French. The oldest engines found included Austrian small-switch 0-6-0's, stamped 1865, while the newest were marked 1944.

Near Paris we captured a German execution train, used to transport Jews to isolated country spots and asphyxiate them. The train consisted of sixty-five boxcars, each sealed tight by tar paper. The gas entered the car through a small pipe. No bodies were found, but the characteristic stench of corpses indicated that the train had recently been used.

Although captured railway stock has been an important asset, the bulk of our equipment came from the U. S. under a ferrying program that was declared fantastic when originally broached in 1942. Hundreds of steam and Diesel locomotives were shipped to England, readied for operations, stored. What was really revolutionary was the prefabrication in the States of twenty thousand boxcars, gondolas, cabooses. They were manufactured especially for Continental railroads. The cars are smaller than American models; they have four wheels instead of eight, and a different coupling mechanism, which allows them to be used with captured stock. The knocked-down cars, like the locomotives, had been sent to England, assembled there by the same railway outfits that were to use them on the Continent, and, after the invasion had started, ferried across the Channel on barges, LST's and "seatrains"—ocean-going freighters especially constructed to carry railway cars.

Getting rail lines and equipment into shape was a sizable job, but the biggest headaches came when trains began to move. The crux of the problem was this: The first trains were the most crucial, for they supplied priority cargo to armies on the move. They had to run long before complete railway facilities could be provided—there was no time to wait for communication lines to be installed, fuel and water points to be repaired or sidings to be rebuilt.

The trains moved on the heels of Engineer gangs—as soon as a section of rail was repaired, the cars rolled. When telephone lines hadn't been strung, jeep couriers dashed between dispatch points with orders for the trains. If a courier was knocked off by a sniper, the trains were stalled for hours. Some coal and water facilities had been left standing by the Germans, but most of them had been damaged or destroyed. Thrown on their own resources, our men foraged the countryside for timber. They dipped water out of ditches, streams, shell craters, and organized civilian bucket brigades. Sometimes there wasn't time to provision a train with all necessary equipment before it had to depart. In the blackout, when lanterns hadn't been furnished, the brakemen signaled with lighted magazines, the flames of cigarette lighters, or glowing cigarette butts.

Even after communication and fuel and water facilities were installed, and regular schedules instituted, a maze of operational problems still continued to bedevil the railway outfits. The demands on the railways were so large that sometimes trains were overloaded, which caused them to stall. This necessitated cutting the train in half and pulling each section into the first available siding. The sidings were frequently far apart, and by the time the engine returned to pick up the second section, later trains—dispatched as frequently as every thirty minutes from the station—were piling up for miles down the track. The short-range solution was more sidings. But they took time to build. The long-range solution, in the case of double-track lines where only a single track was operating, was to repair both tracks—allowing more trains, and shorter ones, to run. This required even more time.

Finally, the accidents of combat inevitably disrupted the best-laid plans. Communications were a particular problem. Telephone contact frequently had to depend on a single line, strung by Signal Corps men under intermittent harassing by shellfire and snipers. German soldiers, caught in rear areas after the tide of battle had swept forward, frequently cut the line. With the line out, a jeep courier had to be rushed between dispatch points with orders for the trains. It was bad enough when things got snarled on a double-track line, but with a single-track road, with loaded trains heading one way and empties going the other, it took hours to back cars down the line, switch them to sidings, and unravel the tangle.

Trains operated within five miles of the front lines. During the early part of July the first railway line—from Cherbourg to Carentan and Lison—paralleled the German front along almost its entire length. Each time a train passed, the German 88's opened up. This went on steadily, morning and evening, for two weeks. And the enemy's guns are not the only danger if trains get too close to the front—Allied supply trains have accidentally been bombed by Allied planes.

Combat pressure has inevitably led to the abandonment of every sort of railroad

At an assembly line for the Transportation Corps rolling stock in England, the crane on the left inverts a completed under-structure while the crane on the right hoists a car end at the beginning of the car "out" line. (10-17-44)

precedent. Back home, the Interstate Commerce Commission fines a railroad a thousand dollars if any man is kept on duty for more than sixteen hours. On our military roads, a man isn't considered to have served his apprenticeship until he's been on a continuous run for at least thirty-two hours. The crews live, eat, sleep on the trains. They bed down in boxcars while the trains are stalled or unloading, eat while they work, take their leisure in banter with civilians lining the track.

But the trains get through. A little over a month after D-day, they were running down the Cotentin peninsula. Shortly after the city's liberation, our men were operating the Paris railroad yards—yards that are reputedly more intricate than Chicago's. In the same swift, impromptu fashion, TC railroaders and truckers expect to make Berlin.

Sgt. Oliver W. Morss of Jasper, OR, uses a Belgian railwayman's curved horn to signal the engineer, while Pvt. Donald B. Chambers of Los Angeles swings aboard the caboose of a G.I. supply train somewhere in France. (10-9-44)

A U.S. Army-operated express train arriving in Paris from Cherbourg, France. (1-24-45)

A lifting beam is lowered into position for attachment to a locomotive aboard the seatrain *Texas* at Birkenhead, England. (7-31-43)

A diesel is loaded in an English port for Channel crossing to France. Transportation Corps personnel conditioned these locomotives in English-loaned shops in Britain. (9-10-44)

Enlisted men of the
751st Railway Shop
Battalion reassemble a
diesel engine after ship-
ment to Britain.
(2-10-44)

Pvt. Leon A. Kaczmarek, Bayonne,
NJ, stencils the Transportation Corps
symbol on a completed box car at
the assembly line in Hainault, Ilford,
England. (10-17-44)

A good comparison of relative sizes can be seen as a British switch engine, or PUG, moves a U.S.-built locomotive and tender at Queens Dock, Glasgow, Scotland. (4-30-43)

A GMC truck was converted into a standard-gauge shunter. It was used in warehouses to avoid a fire hazard. (4-14-43)

At Ashchurch, England, Cpl. "Big John" Baraniak, Port Ready, NY, engineers this switch engine made from a GMC truck. (6-16-43)

A 27-year veteran of the Union Pacific Rail-road, Sgt. Frank L. Stinson, Nampa, ID, volunteered for duty shortly after his son, James, was killed in action aboard a U.S. carrier at Guadalcanal. (10-12-43)

Sgt. Dan F. Terry, Hamlet, NC, throws a switch for T/5 Arthur Bakken, Crookston, MN, at Newbury, England. (11-8-43)

Huge quantities of railroad, highway and other transportation supplies wait the large-scale Allied invasion of Nazi-held Europe. In the center are American Diesel locomotives and gasoline tank cars. To the left is a British locomotive and goods wagons. British Isles. (4-7-44)

A trainload of American M3 light tanks, called "Honeys" by the British, are shown with British troops. (1943)

Known as the Warwell car, these specially built flat cars are shown loaded with General Grant tanks at an Ordnance Depot somewhere in England. The tanks were drained of fuel and loaded with unit equipment for shipment to the front line. (2-4-43)

A view illustrating the industrial might that the U.S. brought to the Allied war effort. This huge stockpile of locomotives is shown at Penrhos Junction, Caerphilly, Wales. (4-7-44)

This was the view at the railroad yards of Alençon, France. The yards had been bombed by Amercan aircraft to prevent the Germans from utilizing the railroad facilities to aid their escape from the American advance. (8-22-44)

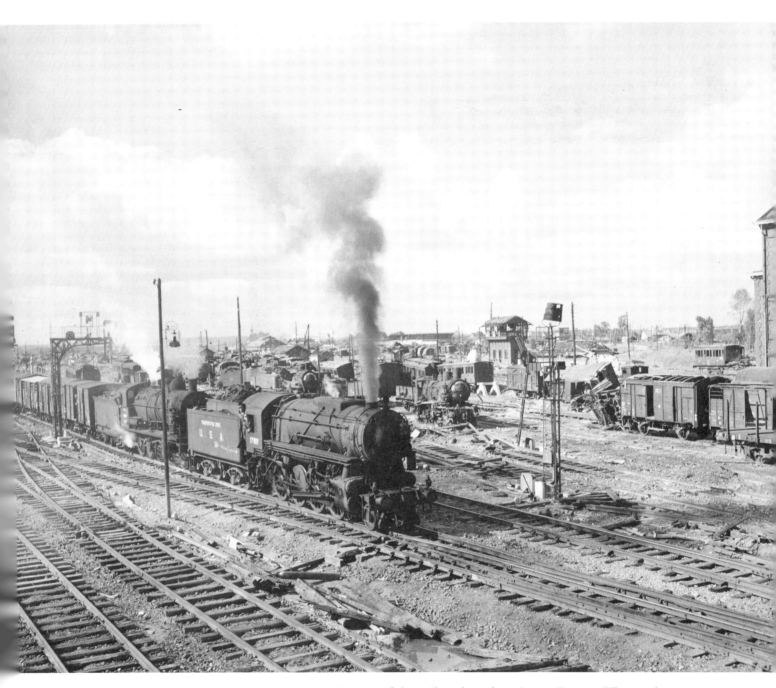

An American engine with G.I. crew pulls out of the railroad yards at Laon, France. The yard had been damaged by American bombing during the German occupation. (10-9-44)

This riddled locomotive in the railroad yards at Mantes, France, was one of over 500 cars and engines lost by the Germans in the early spring 1944 American air forces offensive. (8-19-44)

With no electric power available, French manpower was used to turn U.S. Army #2208 on the turntable at Chartres, France. (8-25-44)

A crew of the 2nd Railroad Battalion servicing a locomotive in facilities they have refurbished at Carentan, France. (7-12-44)

French trainmen shunt trains, loaded with American equipment for the French army, into rail yards at Cherbourg, France. (3-19-45)

Pvts. Robert Losey, Kent City, MI, and Charles H. Wise, Baltimore, MD, guard a loaded train as it leaves a French-guarded railway yard on its way to the front. (1-17-45)

A train operated by the 729th Railroad Operating Battalion leaving Cherbourg on a regular scheduled run to Carentan, France, with Allied soldiers and French civilians aboard. (7-31-44)

Without electric power the Americans use a bulldozer to move this French turntable. (7-15- 44)

Men of the 729th Railway Operating Battalion recovered this U.S. locomotive originally brought to France in 1917. The engine was repaired in Cherbourg and placed in service moving matériel. (7-13-44)

In Bensdorf, France, 1st Sgt. Herman Warner, Sacramento, CA, is photographed riding the vehicle which was used to test track gauge after repair. (12-3-44)

Three U.S. railroads contributed to this group working in France. Left to right: Sgt. L.F. Budasky, Meadville, PA (Erie Railroad); Pvt. J.C. Calcaterra, Herrin, IL (The Pennsylvania); Pvt. K. Smith, Columbus, OH (The Pennsylvania); Sgt. S.M. White, Rockingham, NC (Atlantic Coast Line); and Pvt. P. Weldon, Boston, MA (fireman atop tender).

The Corptet-Louvet Locomotive Works in Paris was placed under contract by the U.S. Army Transportation Corps to repair locomotives and make parts. Here a set of driving wheels is being turned. (5-2-45)

Typical Yank ingenuity is exemplified in this delapidated French gasoline handcar rigged in Briey, France, by T/Sgt. J. Gray, Taylorville, IL, T/Sgt. A. Kruszewski, Philadelphia, PA, T/Sgt. A. Nunn, Rock Hill, SC, T/5 J.J. Zumda, Detroit, MI, and T/5 W. Avery, Red Wing, MN. (10-23-44)

There was no power for this trolley inside the Maginot Line, but that didn't stop this group of G.I.'s from trying out the novel method of transport. (9-15-44)

The "Toot Sweet Express," operated by the 728th Railway Operating Battalion in Cherbourg France, was always run by a French engineer and supervised by an American engineer. Emile Hainneville and American engineer Ruel L. Crutchfield, Mt. Sidney, VA, are shown. (2-10-45)

Pfc. Charles E. Frost, Bolt Hill, Eliot, ME and T/5 Raul Ruschkofski, Loganport, IN, are shown packing bearings in Cherbourg, France. (2-10-45)

"Toot Sweet Express" crewman Cpl. A. Judd, Portland, ME, T/5 R.L. Crutchfield, Mt. Sidney, VA, and 2nd Lt. C.P. Burks, Indianapolis, IN, are given final instructions by Lt. Col. C.D. Love, Louisville, KY. (2-10-45)

The Battignolles railroad yards in Paris. (1-24-45)

Cpl. Robert D. Baer, Tuscarawas, OH, yardmaster at the Battignolles Railyards in Paris. (5-24-45)

Flat cars, carrying medium tanks headed for the front, are inspected by Capt. Francis J. De Pauw at Marseilles, France. (2-10-45)

These freight cars in Verdun, France, contain crushed rock which is to be used as a foundation for a quartermaster depot. (12-3-44)

Stationmaster Sgt. Melvin R. Holmberg of Minneapolis, MN, is shown with flat-car loads of damaged equipment ready for transport some-where in France. (8-1-44)

Maj. T.O. Seiberling (Bonneterre, MO), Capt. H.J. Martin (Wellington, KS), Lt. Col. F.L. Oliphant (Des Moines, IA), Capt. T.L. Adams (Las Vegas, NV) and Capt. A.S. Kemp (Valley Stream, NY) pose while examining seals on box cars in Paris. The destination markings were obliterated from the photo by the Army censor before release. (2-15-45)

T/4 Toni Kloske, Milwaukee, WI, christens the first "fast freight." The trains carried priority goods from Cherbourg to Paris. (1-21-45)

A view of one of the platforms inside the Main Station at Frankfurt, Germany, where despite repeated bombings, the roof structure survived, although not a single piece of glass remained. (4-4-46)

Photographed at the Brittany Base Section, Rennes, France, this captured German tank car was believed to have been used to carry hydrogen peroxide, "a liquid explosive for the robot bomb," better known as the V-2 rocket. (12-11-44)

The first French diesel passenger train readied to resume service in France is taken on a trial run somewhere in Brittany. T/Sgt. Herman McCrimmon, Southern Pines, NC, is at the controls. (9-6-45)

Sgt. Charles Howell, Haleyville, AL, and Pvt. Albert Childress, Memphis, TN, both of the 120th Railway Operation Battalion, man this Army diesel in Lison, France. (8-1-44)

A Transportation Corps train moving across the Rhine at Wesel, Germany, on a bridge constructed by the U.S. 9th Army Engineers. (4-10-45)

V

On to Berlin!

In its performance overseas in 1944, the Military Railway Service clearly proved the value of its months of preparation for the job of keeping the supply lines open and materials of war moving forward to meet the demands of the battlefront. Through such performance, American railway men and railway materials played their part in bringing victory nearer and in pushing the war home to the enemy. By early March 1945 American troops looked down upon the Rhine River and across to Hitler's Germany. The question on everyone's mind was how the Allies were going to bridge that wide river, especially when German soldiers were firmly entrenched nearby.

Allied plans for bridging the Rhine originally called for the erection of the first railway bridge at Duisburg, Duesseldorf or Cologne. After the capture of the Remagen railway bridge on March 7, 1945, immediate steps were taken to fix the damaged lines leading to that bridge from the west bank. Ten days later the bridge collapsed without warning and this forced the MRS to return to its original plan. The only good location was at Wesel, and there, on April 8, the first railway bridge was completed. That effort took less than 10 days. By V-E Day the eastbound freight over the Wesel bridge amounted to 273,141 long tons consisting primarily of food and ammunition.

The Wesel railway bridge involved construction of a 1,752-foot single-track span over the Rhine River, the laying of approximately two miles of connecting track, and the preparation of the required yard facilities at Wesel and Buederich. The 717th Railway Operating Battalion Detachment repaired track at the two yards and laid track over the bridge. The Engineers assisted in constructing the line from the Buederich Yard to the west side of the bridge and in building turnouts at the approaches to the bridge. The 729th Railway Operating Battalion transported rail and construction materials and furnished a 24-hour switching service with six diesel-electric locomotives. On April 9, 1945, the 720th Railway Operating Battalion moved the first train across the river. In April alone, the MRS operated 4,287 freight trains, which carried forward 1,926,947 long tons of supplies and equipment, for a total of 329,813,897 ton-miles throughout Germany. The average load for a single car was 13.6 tons. In April the MRS also ran 108 hospital trains, 278 prisoner trains, 71 troop trains, 97 leave trains, and 93 refugee trains over this bridge.

By May 14, 1945, the Military Railway Service organization on the European continent consisted of the following: 1 general headquarters, 2 headquarters and headquarters companies, 7 railway grand divisions, 24 railway operating battalions, 7 railway shop battalions, 8 military police battalions and 2 separate military police companies, 2 base depot companies, 1 railway transportation company, 5 railway workshops (mobile), and 10 hospital train maintenance detachments.

When V-E Day was announced on May 8, the MRS was using bridges across the river at Duisburg, Worth, Ludwigshafen-Mannheim, Mainz and Wesel. More than a dozen lines were open and operating. Supplies flowed into railheads near Leipzig, Nuremburg, Regensberg, Munich, Magdeburg and Brunswick.

With the end of hostilities, the direction and character of railway traffic changed abruptly. There was temporary congestion while the necessary adjustments were made. The forward movement of freight was drastically curtailed, and the great bulk of U.S. Army personnel began moving out of the theater. In addition to the outbound American troops, the railways carried large numbers of German prisoners and displaced persons. All this activity placed a heavy strain on the limited supply of railway equipment, even though some relief was provided by equipment received from the United States and by the repair and utilization of much captured German rolling stock.

Berlin, which formerly had excellent rail connections with western Germany, was almost isolated at the end of the war. For the support of the British and American personnel in that city, the Soviet authorities made available only a single-track railway with no signal facilities. It ran from Berlin to a truck transfer point at Helmstedt and was operated by German civilians under Soviet supervision. The first U.S. supply train entered Berlin on July 27, 1945. Railway service between Berlin and Helmstedt was unsatisfactory, the slow-moving cargoes were often pilfered, and the Soviet officials proved generally uncooperative.

The main task facing the Military Railway Service in the summer and autumn of 1945 was the removal of men and matériel from the theater. The job had to be done in spite of personnel losses due to redeployment and demobilization. The staff of the MRS spent the greater part of June 1945 assembling approximately 2,000 passenger cars and the necessary motive power for the movement of redeployed personnel from railheads in Germany to the Reims assembly area in France, and from there to Marseille, Le Havre and Antwerp. Because of the inevitable time lag, many officers and men awaiting shipment to the United States or transfer to the Pacific were allowed furloughs, which in turn created a competing demand for rail transportation. In July 1945 General Gray reported that an "unbelievable total" of 1,729 cars was being used for leave and redeployment travel. In order to provide the maximum lift, the MRS carried 1,000 soldiers or more per train, as compared with about 500 in the U.S. during the peak period of the war. Obviously, good service was impossible.

With its wartime mission ended and demobilization in full swing, General Headquarters, MRS, was closed on October 24, 1945, and General Gray relinquished his post as Director General. That month MRS troops were withdrawn from the Belgian railways and plans were laid to turn over the German railways to civilian control under the American military government. Upon the departure, General Gray turned his command over to General Burpee.

The following article originally appeared in the June 30, 1945, issue of *Railway Age*. "German Railways at the End of the War", provides the reader with an interesting insight into the enemy's rail systems during World War II. The story was written by Colonel John W. Wheeler, XVI Corps of Engineers, 9th U.S. Army.

Commanding Officer of the MRS, Brig. Gen. Carl R. Gray Jr., St. Paul, MN, greets hometowners Cpt. Michael Gabriel and Pfc. Sidney Wissenzweig at a railroad yard in Belgium. The just-dedicated engine had been named for Pvt. Harold J. O'Brien, St. Paul, one of 17 railroad men killed in action. (2-27-45)

Supply trains roll across the Robert Gouldin railway bridge over the Rhine River. The engineers of the Advance Section Communication Zone completed the bridge and approaches in 10 days. (4-10-45)

German Railways at the End of the War

By Col. John W. Wheeler
XVI Corps of Engineers, 9th U.S. Army

The ability of the German Railways to continue to operate under terrific air attack prolonged the war for many months. Without this highly trained organization and excellent system Hitler could not have carried on his fanatical final twelve months of war.

Over long periods of time the Allied air forces reported destroying great numbers of locomotives, cars, bridges, yards, and terminals, but to our surprise the enemy kept on rolling. At every station there appeared this sign, "Raden mussen rollen fur den Sieg" (Wheels must turn for the victory). Even the railroads could not roll him to victory but, to the astonishment of all, when the Ruhr industrial district was captured there were found there and in Westphalia, just south of the Ruhr, hundreds of locomotives in good condition and thousands of cars—box cars, flats, gondolas, new refrigerators, coaches, and sleeping cars. True, the enemy had robbed the railroads of France, Belgium, and Holland but, even so, his losses were terrific over a period of months and he still had motive power and cars aplenty when the end came. The railways were finally put out of business by Allied air forces by cutting rail in enough places to prevent repair and thereby pen up the equipment until attacking ground forces could overrun it.

The great majority of the railways in Germany are under the control of the Deutche Reichsbahn, or German State Railway, and the subdivisions will be noted as similar to ours. Even before the advent of the Nazi government, Germany was to a great extent regimented, and close government control over railways was a part of their ever-growing war scheme. It appears that individual enterprise in Germany had been killed and success could only be attained through state authority. This is directly opposite from our experience with railways in two wars. Under government control in the first war our roads made a poor showing as against the efficient performance in this war under individual operation and voluntary cooperation.

Maintenance Excellent

In the final days of the struggle, after the writer's Corps had crossed the Rhine and attacked the Ruhr Valley, the enemy destroyed very nearly all of his railway bridges, and on the Rhine he accomplished total destruction. All bridges, such as the one at Dusseldorf, were destroyed beyond repair. On the whole, Germany's railway bridges were equal to those of any nation and superior to many.

. . . It seemed to us on the scene of the action that the German military were equally enraged at the Allied armies and their own people who chose to stay in the invaded sections.

Even after six years of war, with accompanying man-power shortage, German railway maintenance was excellent. Few people have seen better ballasting and surfacing than existed right up to the final surrender . . . . Ballast is generally broken stone or slag. Both are abundant in Germany and on short haul from the source. Germany has used with more success the steel tie than has any other nation. The writer feels that our treated wood ties are better, but knowledge of German success with steel is worth remembering when and if wood ties become scarce. Wood ties both treated and untreated are used on certain sections. Their joint fastening is intricate in comparison to ours . . . this no doubt results from the use of the double tie at joints and the desire to keep their number to a minimum.

Rail sections are similar to ours and weights of rail used are lighter because of lighter axle loads. Their cars are generally considered to have 20-ton capacity against our 40, and their locomotives lighter in weight approaching the same ratio.

Freight equipment, although lighter and smaller, is quite good. Special-type cars, built to accommodate special commodities, are more common than in the United States. Couplers are of the regular continental type used in practically all nations except in America. The gauge is standard.

In some sections narrow gauge is still in use, and a system of dollies is used to transport standard-gauge cars over narrow-gauge track. To pass narrow-gauge cars over standard-gauge track the same additional rail is used as in the United States. Passenger equipment is not equal to ours but is quite satisfactory, considering that passenger hauls are much shorter than in America. Horizontal curvature is easy and compares favorably with ours. Gradient is held to our standards with extensive use of tunnels in rough topography.

Apparently the railway employees were loyal to the Wehrmacht to the final day but, on the other hand, were the most willing class we found to cooperate with us in getting the destroyed system back in operation. We merely repaired the lines we needed for our supply, but the railway people cooperated heartily and seemed anxious to get their lines back in operation.

After the Rhine River crossing, the writer's Corps attacked and cleared up the Ruhr industrial district and remained there after so doing to govern temporarily that district. If you can imagine the Calumet steel district from Waukegan through South Chicago to Michigan City with every railroad bridge demolished as well as highway crossings, all yards a mass of twisted rails, craters, skeletons of cars, and wrecks of locomotives and then look at the steel plants and locomotive works if Essen there in front of you with nothing but huge piles of debris to mark the spot of such institutions as the proud and mighty Krupp Works, you must wonder how long it will take to rebuild what was once a great nation. Germany was a railway-minded nation using many tramways adjacent to highways for heavy hauling.

Truly, Germany was a great nation of efficient people and natural resources underlaid with a lust to conquer and rule by force. She has finally paid for her folly in a destroyed nation. The red board is against her now, it will gradually change to yellow, but those of us who saw the destruction doubt the appearance of the green light for many decades.

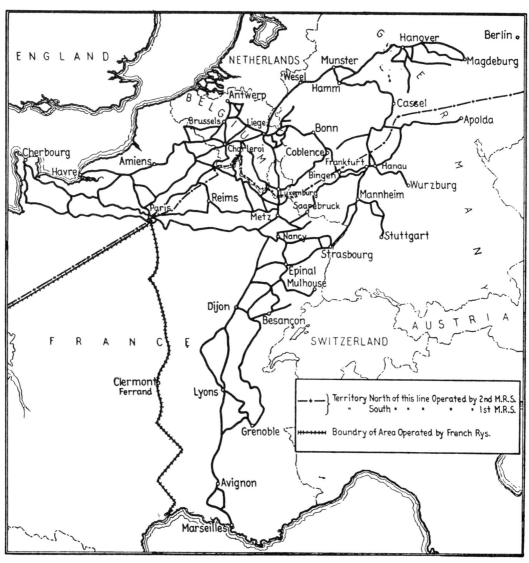

The European railways which were being operated by the Military Railway Service when the war ended.

G.I.'s repairing a leaky valve on an old German tank in the Mehlen, Germany, railroad yards. The tank cars unloaded their gasoline into storage tanks through a pipeline across the Rhine, from which the gasoline fueled the 1st Army drive into Germany. (4-9-45)

This German engine, operated by T/4 Steward Weifon, Beckley, WV, and T/5 Leon Radomski, Chicago, IL, was the first engine to operate from east of Frankfurt. (4-20-45)

A string of Navy pontoons, guided by U.S. Army Engineers being lowered onto flat cars by a Lorain 82-30 ton lift crane, were used in the construction of the "Lincoln on the Hudson" railway bridge across the Rhine River, Germany. The background was obliterated by military censors. (3-25-45)

These three locomotives were among 50 locomotives and 750 freight cars captured at Darmstadt, Germany, by the 4th Armored Division of the 3rd U.S. Army. (3-25-45)

Pfc. Lewis Miller, Chattanooga, TN, and T/Sgt. Robert Singer, Latrobe, PA, break a valve on a 2-8-2 camouflaged German engine. (4-20-45)

T/5 C.E. Fiske, Poplar Bluffs, MS, and T/5 A.H. Haines, Flat Woods, KY, working on one of 17 German locomotives repaired by the 746th Railway Operations Battalion within four days of taking over this roundhouse. (4-19-45)

After their capture, the Karl Alexander mines at Baesweile, Germany, produced coal for the Allied advance. (11-18-44)

Destroyed by the retreating Germans, this new bridge was built by the 33rd Engineers of the 30th Division. (12-16-44)

The roundhouse and turntable at the Mayen, Germany, yards were left intact when the Germans retreated. Many locomotives with their steam down were found unmoved. (3-12-45)

This train, carrying a French 340mm gun used by the Germans, was captured intact by U.S. 7th Army in Eberbach, Germany. (4-13-45)

Lt. Gen. William Simpson, CG of 9th Army, Maj. Gen. Alexander R. Bolling, CG of the 84th Infantry Division, Maj. Gen. Alvin Gillem, CG of the XIII Corps, and Col. A.D. Meads, G-3 with the 9th Army, pose before a captured engine in Arendsee, Germany. (4-17-45)

This turntable was manually operated by the 309th Combat Engineers, aided by displaced Polish citizens. The engine was used to convey supplies between Arendsco and Oebisfelde, Germany, for the 9th Army. (4-26-45)

"The Berlin Express," shown at Oschersleben, Germany, carried ammunition for use by the 970th Quartermaster Service Company, XIX Corps, U.S. 9th Army. (4-16-45)

Soldiers of the 82nd Airborne Division, U.S. 15th Army, ready to board box cars at Duren, Germany, bound for northern Germany. (4-26-45)

Two U.S. Army locomotives passing over a rebuilt viaduct to pick up a string of cars filled with gasoline, near Stolberg, Germany. (2-16-45)

Capt. William McCormick, Savannah, GA, and Cpl. Stanley Bourgeois, New Bedford, MA, supervise maintenance of the right of way at the Bremen, Germany, Port Command. (7-30-45)

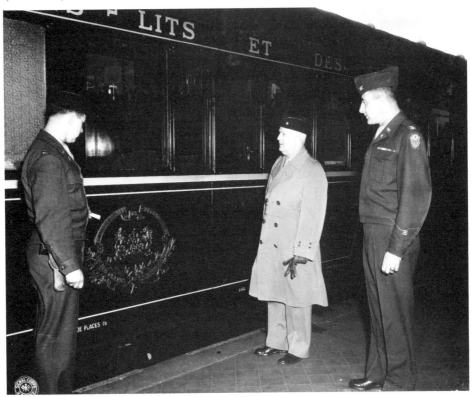

Brig. Gen. Thomas Bresnahan, Capt. George Smith, and Col. William Ghormley inspect a new train before its run between Bremerhaven and Frankfurt. It was assembled from the former "Blue Express" which had run between Constantinople and Paris. (4-25-46)

Under the supervision of the MRS, operations of the Amingaon-Pandu railway ferry of the Bengal & Assam Railway were carried on at night in Pandu, Assam, India. (12-22-44)

Conclusion

By the end of 1945 the wartime task of the Military Railway Service had practically been completed. In fact, within four months of Germany's surrender, many units had been returned to the United States and "inactivated." Those still overseas were, with a few exceptions, on the alert for orders to board ships to return home. The MRS headquarters in Paris was closed on October 24, and Major General Carl R. Gray Jr., former Director General of the MRS in Europe, arrived in New York with his staff on November 9, continuing directly to St. Paul, Minnesota, where they would be mustered out of active service.

There is little question that American railroad men in Army railway battalions made transportation history during World War II. Although considerable achievements were chalked up in Louisiana, Alaska, North Africa, Italy and Iran, other operations were no less impressive. In India, Burma and the Philippines, the exhibition of skills and stamina by MRS personnel often went far beyond anything their training routine and experience on home railroads had prepared them for.

The main strength of the Army's railroad battalions was concentrated in Europe, supporting the invasion that led to the collapse of Italy and Germany. The story of the Military Railway Service's experiences in Sicily, in the "boot" of Italy, and as the fighting front swept from Normandy across France and the Rhine, deep into Nazi territory, is astounding. Important though the earlier operations were, the most severe test of MRS organization and training was the task of supplying the growing armies as they spread from the beachheads eastward almost to Berlin. For example, Army railroaders were running a flange-wheeled "jeep" on the Cherbourg peninsula 11 days after the first troops went ashore at Normandy. Three months after D-Day the rail lines were open to Paris. In another 30 days the MRS railheads were in Belgium, at Brussels and Liege. Meanwhile, other units coming into the south of France had taken over the lines running from Marseilles up the Rhine Valley, opening up an additional supply route at a time when the limited capacity of the open channel ports made the new route vitally useful.

The Rhine crossing began on March 24, 1945, and less than two weeks later the Wesel bridge had been completed and MRS railroad operations east of the river had begun. On V-E Day the service was using bridges across the Rhine at Duisburg, Worth, Ludwigshafen and Mainz, as well as Wesel.

During the 11 months between D-Day and V-E Day, the Military Railway Service loaded and moved more than 18,500,000 net tons of military materials on lines it operated behind the European battlefronts. From 3,000 tons a day in the early operations in Normandy, its transportation service output rose to 529,275 net tons moved on June 7, 1945, during the period of the Rhine crossings. This was the equivalent of a net ton-mileage of 76,215,456 for the day. On that same June 7th the MRS was operating in the western European area 1,937 locomotives, 34,588 freight cars, and 25,120 miles of track. Its personnel consisted of 1,145 officers, 45 warrant officers, and 25,490 enlisted men, whose overall average civilian railroad experience was 3.06 years per man.

Unlike many of the "fighting" branches of the Army, however, the railroad operating and shop battalions, along with other units organized and trained for specialized technical duties, would not be completely disbanded. The U.S. War Department would continue with a long-range plan, put into effect before hostilities began, whereby suitably organized railway personnel with a high degree of specialized training would be available under company sponsorship for rapid and orderly conversion from civilian to military duties whenever the need arose.

Most of America's largest railroads sponsored one or more railway shops or operating battalions during World War II. Each one of those shops and battalions contributed to the final victory. Unfortunately, the limited space in this book could not chronicle all their remarkable achievements, but one fact is certain: without the courage and deep personal commitment of each of this nation's fighting railroad soldiers, the war would not have concluded in 1945 and hundreds of thousands more lives would have been claimed in the prolonged conflict.

America's soldier-railroaders are to be commended.

Cpl. Thomas Coe, Western Salman, NC, T/5 Marion Evans, Woodland, WA, T/5 Frank Chipak, Cleveland, OH, and S/Sgt. Roy McAfee, Saltello, TX, ride a captured German track bicycle in Bebra, Germany. (4-16-45)

Bibliography

Books by Title

The Battle is the Pay Off, Ralph Ingersoll, 1943.
Crusade in Europe, Dwight D. Eisenhower, 1948.
G.I. Railroader, Chaplain (Captain) R.E. Musser, 1945.
Men of the Erie, Edward Hungerford, 1946.
Railroads at War, S. Kip Farringron Jr., 1944.
Railway Reconstruction in Italy, Royal Engineers, 1946.
Transport for War, Edward Hungerford, 1943.
Victory Rode the Rails, J. Edgar Turner, 1953.

Base Depot Companies, Histories Published

Claiborne & Polk Military Railway (711th Railway Operating Battalion), 1942.
Company A, 713th Railway Operating Battalion, 1946.
Company B, 722nd Railway Operating Battalion, 1946.
Extra 704 West, 1945.
Highlights of History of the 709th Railway Grand Division, 1945.
History of the 706th Railway Grand Division, 1945.
History of the 718th Railway Operating Battalion, 1945.
History of the 756th Railway Shop Battalion, 1945.
Mileposts, 774th Railway Grand Division, 1945.
Pictorial History Headquarters Second Military Railway Service in the E.T.O.
Report of the Engineering Section, 706th Railway Grand Division, 1945.
714th Railway Operating Battalion, 1946.
759th Railway Operating Battalion World War II, 1949.
760th Railway Shop Battalion Diesel, 1945.
765th Railway Shop Battalion, 1947.
The Saga of the 708th, 1947.
The Santa Fe Battalion in World War II, 713 R.O.B., 1946.
The Soldier-Railroaders' Story of the 716th Railway Operating Battalion, 1945.
The 727th Railway Operating Battalion in World War II, 1948.

War Department Publications

Field Manual 55-670, Transportation Corps, Military Railroads and the Military Railway Service, March 27th, 1944.
Historical Report of the Chief Engineer, Including All Operations of the Engine Department, American Expeditionary Forces, 1917-1918, No. 907, July, 1919.
Report of the Chief of Transportation Army Service Forces, World War II, November 30, 1919.
The Engineer Field Manual, Volumes 1 and 2, *Engineer Troops*, 1942.
Report on Military Railway Service in World War II, 1944.

U.S. Army, Department of Publications

History of the Persian Gulf Command, Office of Chief Military History, 1947.
Rail Operations in the Philippines, 1948.
Transportation Corps: Responsibilities, Organization, and Operation, 1951.
Railroads in Defense and War, 1944.
Railway Reconstruction in France, 1947.
Railways of 30 Nations Fighting in Europe, 1948.

Index